THE UNIVERSITY OF WALES

AN ILLUSTRATED HISTORY

THE UNIVERSITY OF WALES

AN ILLUSTRATED HISTORY

GERAINT H. JENKINS

UNIVERSITY OF WALES PRESS
CARDIFF 1993

© University of Wales, 1993

All rights reserved. No part of this book may be reproduced, stored in a retrieval system, or transmitted, in any form or by any means, electronic, mechanical, photocopying, recording or otherwise, without clearance from the University of Wales Press, 6 Gwennyth Street, Cardiff CF2 4YD

ISBN 0-7083-1223-3

British Library Cataloguing in Publication Data

A catalogue record for this book is available from the British Library

Typeset in Wales by Megaron, Cardiff
Printed in Wales by Gwasg Dinefwr, Llandybïe
Cover design by Design Principle, Cardiff

To all Students and Staff
– past and present –
of the
University of Wales

Preface

This book was undertaken on the initiative of members of the Council of the University of Wales who invited me to prepare a popular and attractive, illustrated volume which would offer a lively overview – in the form of extended captions – of the most significant and interesting features of life within the University of Wales over the past hundred years. As a graduate of the University and a historian in the oldest of its constituent Colleges, I gladly accepted the commission and I hope my portrait of the period will appeal not only to those who are closely associated with academic life in Wales but also to the lay public at large. The content of a pictorial history is, of course, principally determined by the largely haphazard survival of photographic records and my guiding principle of selection in hunting for material was to assemble prints and photographs of strong historical and visual interest. During my visits to various archives in the University Registry, the constituent Colleges and elsewhere, it soon became apparent that some collections are richer and more abundant than others, and this is reflected in the final selection of photographs.

In many ways, this has been a collective enterprise and I owe much to the generous help of institutions and individuals. I am deeply grateful to archivists and administrative assistants in the University of Wales Registry and in each of the constituent Colleges for their valuable advice and assistance. The staff of the National Library of Wales have been immensely helpful in supplying material and answering queries. I should like in particular to express my sincere appreciation and gratitude to the following individuals who have assisted me in various ways: Catrin Bevan, David A. Bevan, Frank Bott, Richard Brinkley, Joan Bullingham, Jên Dafis, Lyn Lewis Dafis, Olwen Daniel, Roger Davies, Russell Davies, Gareth Wyn Evans, William Howells, Huw Flynn Hughes, Brian James, David Jenkins, Stuart John, John Wyn Jones, Alan Kemp, John M. Lancaster, D. Gareth Lewis, Barbara Parry, D. T. W. Price, S. J. Pritchard, Lona Roberts, Tomos Roberts, Ian Salmon, Chris Turner, Rosie Waite, Lynn E. Williams and Robin H. Williams. Dr E. L. Ellis, Dr Prys Morgan and Professor Emeritus J. Gwynn Williams were kind enough to read the text in draft and to save me from several blunders and infelicities. Carys Briddon worked wonders by transforming my messy manuscript into immaculate typescript, and I am indebted to Delyth Fletcher for her secretarial help. Susan Jenkins of the University of Wales Press suggested further improvements with characteristic tact and understanding, and also expertly guided the volume through the press. I should also like to thank Ned Thomas, Director of the University of Wales Press, for his keen interest in this project. Any errors, inadequacies and omissions which remain are, of course, of my own making. Last, but by no means least, my sincere thanks go to my wife and children for cheerfully coping with the disruption of domestic life which research and writing increasingly provokes in this hectic age.

Aberystwyth   Geraint H. Jenkins

ALTHOUGH Queen Victoria reigned for sixty-four years – longer than any other British monarch – she spent only seven nights in Wales and usually referred to her Welsh subjects with ill-concealed contempt. Nevertheless, she was never without champions in Wales: *Y Genedl Gymreig* adoringly described her as 'The Great White Mother', and the applause for her was never more enthusiastic than when the Great Seal was affixed to the Royal Charter which constituted the University of Wales on 30 November 1893. This was undoubtedly the crown and summit of the Liberal ascendancy in Wales in the late Victorian era, for the Charter realized a dream which had fired the imagination of the people of Wales since the days of Owain Glyndŵr. The editor of the student magazine of the University College of Wales, Aberystwyth, expressed the sentiments of the whole nation when he declared: 'May it [the University of Wales] flourish like a banyan grove is our pious hope.' The Royal Charter of 1893 (*Plate 1*) now rests in the strongroom of the Registry of the University of Wales in Cardiff.

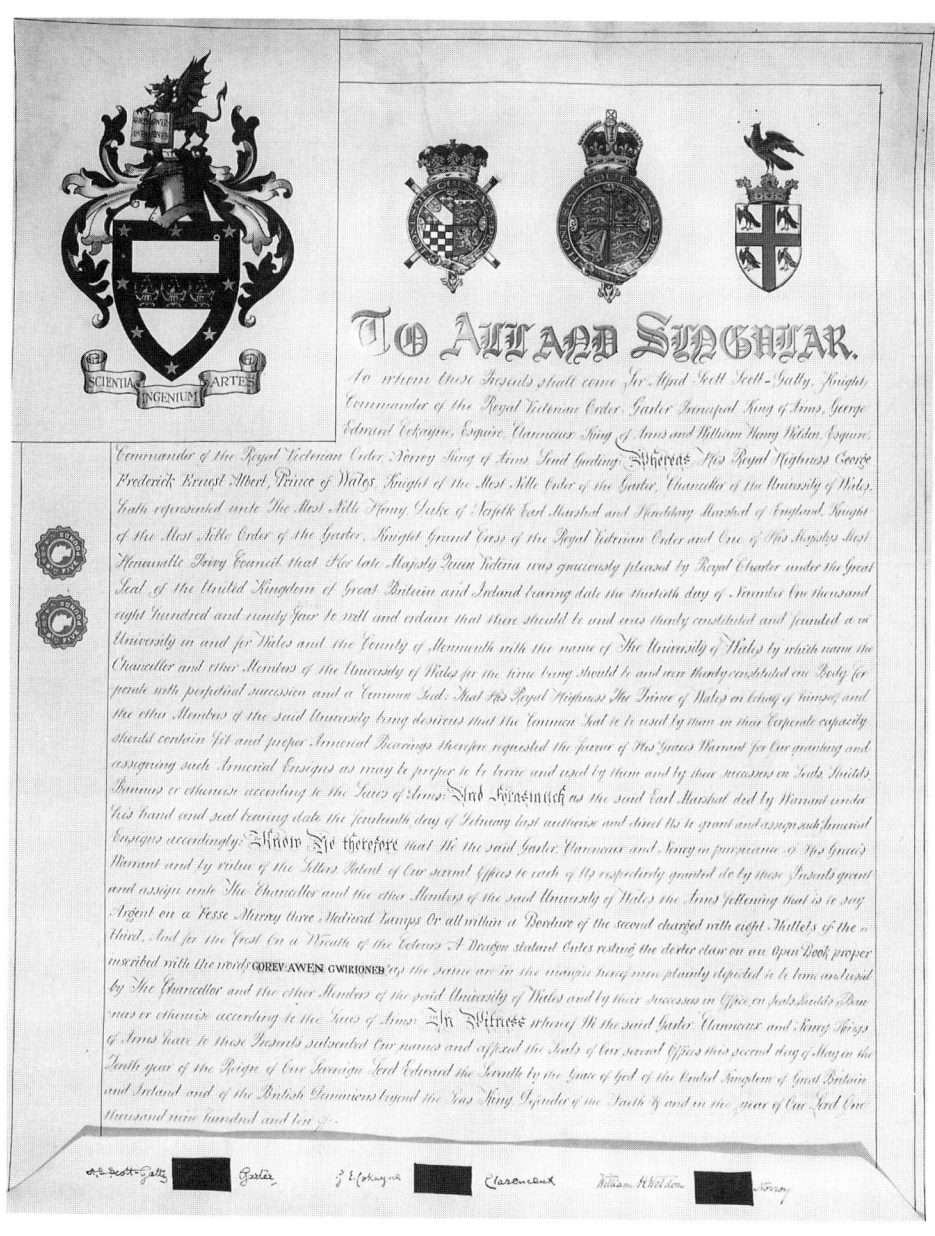

1

During the early stages of drafting and redrafting the Charter, no Welshman was more industrious and resourceful than John Viriamu Jones, Principal of the University College of South Wales and Monmouthshire (*Plate 2*). A native of Pentre-poeth, Swansea, Jones was the son of a Congregationalist minister who, in the hope that his son would become a Christian missionary, had baptized him 'Viriamu', namely the Polynesian rendering of the surname of the missionary John Williams of Erromanga. In fact, Viriamu Jones's gifts were largely scientific, and following a brilliant career at Balliol College, Oxford, and two years' service as Principal of Firth's College, Sheffield, he was invited in 1883 to become Principal of the University College of South Wales and Monmouthshire. A frail, delicate, but highly attractive and personable man (Neville Masterman once described him as 'a young Iberian Apollo'), he was much loved by staff and students. Acutely sensible of the principles of nationalism, he strongly believed that in matters of higher education Wales should be the mistress of her own identity, and there is no doubt that the University of Wales owes its existence to his constructive genius. In a celebrated passage, he outlined his vision: 'Scatter iron filings on a sheet of cardboard, they will fall irregularly without trace of ordering. Bring a magnet beneath the cardboard and they will arrange themselves in curves so harmonious and beautiful and mysterious that one never wearies of watching . . . The iron filings are the educational institutions of Wales; and the university, if it plays its part aright, is the magnet that shall link them into an orderly system.' His untimely death, at the age of forty-five, in June 1901 was a calamitous blow for the University of Wales and, according to his widow, 'the people of Wales could not do enough to show their affection for him, and their gratitude'. It is no exaggeration to count him among the principal makers of modern Wales.

2

ALTHOUGH Thomas Charles Edwards (*Plate 3*), Principal of the University College of Wales, Aberystwyth (1872–91), resigned his post before the University of Wales was formally constituted, he played a vital role both in awakening public opinion to the need for a federal university and also in drafting the Charter itself. 'If we are not a nation', he declared in 1896, 'it is because we had no Colleges, no University, to create and cherish our intellectual life. With a National University, we shall make ourselves a nation.' A descendant of Thomas Charles of Bala and son of the theologian, Lewis Edwards, Thomas Charles Edwards had built an immense reputation as a theologian, preacher and exegete prior to his appointment as the first Principal of the University College of Wales, Aberystwyth. On 16 October 1872, assisted by two professors and a registrar-librarian, he had welcomed twenty-six students to the converted hotel which became the first home of 'the people's university', and for nearly twenty years he discharged his functions with tireless efficiency and indomitable optimism. Confronted by lack of funds, personal rivalries and sectarian prejudices, he overcame every obstacle and brought the College through its trials at great cost to his own personal health. When he succeeded his father as Principal of Bala College, he was replaced by Principal T. Francis Roberts, a police sergeant's son who had been first Professor of Greek at the University College of South Wales and Monmouthshire. Like his predecessor, Roberts was a man of the highest integrity who never wavered in his loyalty to the cause of the University of Wales.

THE GOVERNORS of the University College of North Wales, Bangor, took a calculated risk in appointing Harry Rudolf Reichel (*Plate 4*) the first Principal of the College in 1884. A tall, handsome young man of brilliant academic attainments (he could boast four firsts at Balliol College, Oxford), Reichel was a native of Belfast and a churchman of Irish gentry stock who had never visited Wales and was utterly ignorant of its language and traditions. It was a most improbable appointment. But the gamble proved a resounding success, for Reichel served as Principal for forty-three years and won universal respect for his integrity, firm principles and selfless dedication to the College. A reserved, courteous and modest man, he gave the impression of being a rather cold fish, and students certainly found him a forbidding figure. Most of them dreaded his invitations to breakfast, for the Principal usually passed around the food and then ate in stony silence. Yet he was a cultivated, cosmopolitan man who was particularly fond of poetry and music. On one memorable occasion, to the piano accompaniment of Sir Walford Davies, he sang 'Widdicombe Fair' with great gusto! Reichel also served the University of Wales with great distinction. He worked in harness with Viriamu Jones to produce a draft charter and in due course served as Vice-Chancellor of the University of Wales on six separate occasions. Until his death, aged seventy-four, at Biarritz in June 1931, Sir Harry Reichel (he was knighted in 1907) remained devoted to the highest ideals of the University of Wales.

4

IT COULD be argued that Sir Herbert Isambard Owen (*Plate 5*) was the true architect of the University of Wales, for it was he who piloted the Charter movement through the murky waters of university and government life in the early 1890s. Every minute detail of academic business and university statutes was at his fingertips, and Lord Aberdare rightly asserted that 'no trained draftsman could have shown more skill' in the framing of the charter. A consultant physician by calling, he was never happier than when drafting briefs or compiling minutes. No one was better acquainted with the administrative and technical problems of the federal university and when he was appointed Senior Deputy Chancellor in 1895 he became virtually the 'working head' of the University. He brought great dignity to University degree ceremonies and other functions. Thomas Richards recalled his 'dignified presence, his sonorous and penetrating diction [and] the cultured Latinity of the ceremonial words'. His unsmiling manner and fussy concern for legal niceties were not to everyone's taste, but he served the University of Wales splendidly until his death in Paris in January 1927.

5

THE TORTOISE-LIKE progress of the draft charter committee, which deliberated in strict secrecy in the Raven Hotel, Shrewsbury, on a number of occasions in 1891–3, both intrigued and infuriated the Welsh press. 'If length of deliberation were always an infallible sign of the wisdom of the conclusions arrived at', sighed the editor of the *Western Mail*, 'the charter committee would be entitled to plume itself very highly upon what it has accomplished.' Isambard Owen was a stickler for detail and clauses were deliberated upon, altered, amended, withdrawn and reinstated with tedious regularity (*Plate 6*). Lord Aberdare had good cause to quote Dryden in describing the final draft as 'not the product of a day, but the well-ripened fruit of wise delay'. The draft charter was finally adopted by members of the University Conference at Shrewsbury on 6 January 1893. Its contents were then subjected to detailed public scrutiny before being forwarded to the Privy Council and Parliament. The constitution was based on the federal principle: each of the three constituent colleges was an equal member of the University and a degree-conferring body, and the Crown was empowered to increase that number by a Supplemental Charter. The governing authorities were to be the Crown as Visitor, a Chancellor, a University Court, a Vice-Chancellor, a University Senate and a Guild of Graduates. To Viriamu Jones and his colleagues, the University Charter signalled the intellectual coming of age of Wales.

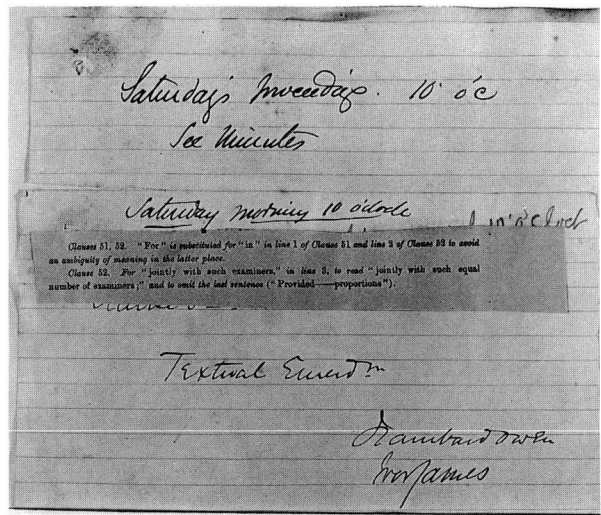

6

ON 6 APRIL 1894 the University Court – which Principal Viriamu Jones liked to call 'the Educational Parliament of Wales' – met for the first time in a poorly lit and rather dingy Privy Council chamber in Whitehall (*Plate 7*). Lord Rosebery, the Prime Minister, chaired the meeting and was accompanied by Arthur Acland, Minister of Education, and Sir Charles Lennox-Peel, Clerk of the Council. When the photographer for the *Black and White* magazine arrived, not a few of the assembled members began preening themselves, shifting their chairs, and even standing up in order to enable the camera to record their presence for posterity. Among the Welsh dignitaries were Lord and Lady Aberdare, Principal Viriamu Jones, Dr Isambard Owen, T. E. Ellis, Lewis Morris, O. M. Edwards and a number of Members of Parliament. Rosebery was a chilly, melancholic Scotsman who, when dogged by *ennui*, used to cheer himself up by humming 'Rule Britannia'. Whether he did so on this occasion we cannot tell, but an unfortunate reference in his speech to Wales's efforts to place herself on the same footing as 'the older parts' of the kingdom raised a few murmurs of disapproval. He recovered well enough, however, and won the hearts of the assembled throng with a rousing finale: 'I wish with all my heart and in all earnestness to wish you God-speed.'

THE FIRST meeting of the Senate of the University of Wales was held at Aberystwyth on 25–28 September 1894. Often known as 'the second estate', the Senate comprised the three Principals and heads of all the departments in the constituent colleges (*Plate 8*). With tongue in cheek, the editor of the student magazine at Aberystwyth congratulated this august assembly on solving every conceivable problem: 'The senate are believed to have exhausted the resources of logic in their search for truth; all the moods, figures, and fallacies – nay, the hypothetical syllogism itself – have been brought to bear upon the divers weighty questions discussed. No more will the point be raised: "Do we really want a Welsh University?"' Nevertheless, from 1894 until its demise in 1920 the University Senate made more enemies than friends. The abrasive Sir T. Marchant Williams was not alone in believing that it was wasteful and unwieldy, while O. M. Edwards was convinced that it was ill-disposed towards Welsh studies. An anonymous correspondent in *The Times* in February 1896 (it later transpired that his name was Stephen Coleridge of London) pilloried the Senate and Court for frittering away public grants on exorbitant travelling and hotel bills. In his view, the University of Wales was 'a Gastronomic Experiment'!

8

THE 'THIRD estate' in the newly founded federal University was the Guild of Graduates, a convocation which was constituted as part of the Charter of 1893, though its composition was subsequently revised by the provisions of the Supplemental Charter of 1920. The Guild includes as members all graduates and honorary graduates of the University, together with former students of the Welsh Colleges who graduated in any British university prior to 30 November 1895. The aim of the convocation was to enable past and present students to come together in mutual fellowship, to advance the cause of education in Wales, and to foster and support historical and literary research. The Guild held its first meeting at the Raven Hotel, Shrewsbury, on 17 March 1894. Its first Warden was Owen M. Edwards (*Plate 9*), sometime Fellow of Lincoln College, Oxford, and later Chief Inspector at the Welsh Department of the Board of Education. It was his fervent wish that, in the fullness of time, the Guild would become 'the greatest power in Wales'. Such grandiose hopes remained unfulfilled, though it must be said that over the past century the University has benefited enormously from the wise counsel and expertise of its graduates.

9

THE FIRST Welshman to be elected Chancellor of the University of Wales was Henry Austin Bruce, Lord Aberdare (*Plate 10*). Having been the scourge of rioters and trade unionists in Merthyr in his younger days, Lord Aberdare had turned his attention to educational matters in the early 1860s and served as President of the University College of Wales, Aberystwyth (1874–95) and President of the University College of South Wales and Monmouthshire (1884–9). In 1880 he was appointed chairman of the Departmental Committee on Intermediate and Higher Education in Wales and Monmouthshire, and the ensuing Aberdare Report not only formed the basis for the Welsh Intermediate Act of 1889 but also provoked new thinking about the nature of the University of Wales. His was a powerful voice in the council chambers of Wales, and his dignified manner, infinite capacity for taking pains, and gift of chairmanship made him the obvious candidate for the coveted position of Chancellor. When informed of the honour, he wrote to his daughter: 'As I could not reasonably expect to be chosen Archbishop to disestablished Wales, nor to succeed Prince Llewelyn in his temporarily suspended dignity, I feel that Wales could bestow on me no greater honour.' A fortnight later, on 25 February 1895, death robbed the Grand Old Man of the Welsh educational establishment of that honour. There is no reason to believe that the widespread sense of grief which his death occasioned was anything less than genuine, but even so there were not a few who welcomed the opportunity to invite a more eminent figure with royal blood flowing in his veins to serve as Chancellor.

10

THAT 'ROYAL Personage' proved to be no less a person than the heir-apparent, the Prince of Wales (afterwards King Edward VII), who was elected the first of an unbroken line of royal Chancellors in 1895. This was followed by acrimonious exchanges in the University Court as to where the installation ceremony should take place. All were agreed that, as Professor John Rhŷs admitted, 'a great splash' would do wonders for the image of the fledgeling university, but Aberystwyth and Cardiff vied furiously for the right to act as host. Advocates for Cardiff insisted that the largest and most prosperous urban centre in Wales was the most fitting venue for such celebrations, while the case made by Aberystwyth's representatives was based on its historical claim as the 'mother college' and as the undisputed seat of Welsh culture. To the undisguised chagrin of the Cardiff contingent, Aberystwyth won by the margin of four votes.

As if by royal appointment, the sun shone brilliantly on Friday, 26 June 1896, when the royal train (described by awestruck journalists as 'a palace on wheels'), bearing the Prince and Princess of Wales, and accompanied by Princesses Maud and Victoria, ground to a noisy halt at Aberystwyth station at 12.10 p.m. precisely. No expense or effort had been spared to make the visit a success (*Plate 11*). The cruisers HMS *Hermione* and *Bellona*, anchored in the bay, fired a thunderous royal salute, and the Central Wales Choir, conducted by David Jenkins, burst into a rousing chorus of 'The Men of Harlech'. The town, crammed with over 40,000 people, echoed to joyous cheers as the royal carriage, led by the Montgomeryshire Yeomanry, wended its way through the streets which, much to O. M. Edwards's disapproval, were adorned with multi-coloured bunting and Venetian masks rather than the lions of Llywelyn and the dragon of Glyndŵr (*Plate 12*). A spacious and colourfully decorated pavilion had been erected in front of the Town Hall and seven trucks had been hired to convey chairs to accommodate 2,000 guests who represented the academic, aristocratic, clerical, commercial and professional interests of Wales. The ceremony was carried out with great pomp and dignity (*Plate 13*). The Prince was clad in a robe of black satin damask, heavily embroidered with gold and displaying the Welsh dragon in no fewer than five places, while the Princess of Wales wore a scarlet robe trimmed with violet. Ivor James, the Registrar, recited the deed of appointment, handed it to Isambard Owen, the Senior Deputy Chancellor who, in turn, presented it to the Prince. Owen then proceeded to read an address from the University Court before presenting the Chancellor with the insignia of office, the key of the University, the seal, and a copy of the Charter and Statutes. The new Chancellor delighted the assembly by speaking in three tongues (though his voice was described as low and muffled, at least by those located in distant quarters of the marquee) and he won their hearts by declaring an apt God-speed: 'Hir oes a dedwyddwch i chwi oll' (Long life and prosperity to you all). A skittish version of the events was retailed by 'our own Welsh Brer Rabbit' in *Punch*: 'HRH the Prince of Wales, speaking in the language of the Principality, said, "Heddyw Rhag bron ynall pa le bob amser iwodd lyk tobe mae yn dda genyf Y mae yn fyw andsov ery sppri wed Blodeno. Tri Hippippoorar fur der altesse Tywysoges!"' The Chancellor took a keen interest in the proceedings and responded enthusiastically when called upon to bestow an honorary D.Mus. upon his wife, the Princess of Wales, and (to loud cheers) an honorary doctorate of law upon W. E. Gladstone.

The royal party was then cheered along the gaily decorated promenade to the Pier Pavilion, where a splendid luncheon had been prepared for 600 guests.

VISIT OF
H.R.H. the PRINCE OF WALES,
H.R.H. the PRINCESS OF WALES,
AND
T.R.H. the Princesses VICTORIA & MAUD OF WALES.
TO ABERYSTWYTH, JUNE 26th, 1896.

Programme of Proceedings

Installation of H.R.H. the Prince of Wales
AS
Chancellor
OF THE
University of Wales (Prifysgol Cymru.)

Reception in the College
And Luncheon in the Pier Pavilion.

Opening of the Alexandra Hall of Residence
for Women Students
BY
H.R.H. the Princess of Wales.

Grand Evening Concert in the Installation Hall
BY
The Treorky Choir (Conductor—Mr. William Thomas,
The Central Wales Choir (Conductor—Mr. David Jenkins, Mus. Bac.) and
A Band of Harps (Conductor—Mr. F. C. Barker, R.A.M.)

PRICE TWOPENCE.

J. & J. Gibson, Printers, "Cambrian News" Office, Aberystwyth.

11

Lord Rendel presided and the evergreen Gladstone proceeded to upstage the Prince with a cultivated, sentient speech which evoked many cries of 'Hear hear' and 'Go on'. In the afternoon the Princess of Wales opened Alexandra Hall, a new hall of residence for women students. In the evening a stunning display of pyrotechnics rounded off a day of joyous pageantry. In spite of the gloomy forecasts of aggrieved Cardiff citizens, the proceedings passed off with scarcely a hitch. It was a truly memorable occasion, the like of which the ordinary citizens of Aberystwyth had never seen. Even those who counted in Liberal Nonconformist Wales judged it an occasion of the utmost national importance. Llewelyn Williams MP declared, with pardonable exaggeration, that the ceremony was the finest he had ever seen, while Lord Rendel likened it to a coronation which admitted Wales 'into its full inheritance and field of action in the empire and the world at large'. To O. M. Edwards the installation of the new Chancellor was 'a Red Letter Day' in the history of Wales. 'It was a happy day', he wrote. 'If I had to decide which our national day of rejoicing is, I would decide on the twenty sixth of June.' Gallant little Wales had come of age.

13

12

When the Prince of Wales became King Edward VII he ceased to be Chancellor and instead assumed the title of Protector of the University of Wales (1901–10). His son, George, Prince of Wales (later George V) replaced him as Chancellor and was duly installed on 9 May 1902 at Caernarfon Pavilion (*Plate 14*), appropriately, perhaps, under the shadow of the Edwardian castle and not too far from the statue of Sir Hugh Owen. The Prince's address was well received and the cheers were deafening when he spoke of '*our* University'. Indeed, according to one 'country-looking and horny-handed' representative, he had all the makings of 'a superb Association preacher'! There was no building large enough in Bangor to accommodate such substantial numbers of dignitaries and well-wishers, and when the Prince was escorted to lunch in Bangor he was duly informed that, from an architectural point of view, there was little of the College that was worthy of attention. Nine years later the Prince returned as King George V to north Wales for the Investiture of the young Prince of Wales at Caernarfon.

14

IVOR JAMES, first Registrar of the University of Wales, was appointed in March 1895 (*Plate 15*). Formerly Registrar of the University College of South Wales and Monmouthshire, he was a small, dapper man whose absolute devotion to the interests of the University won the admiration of academics and administrators alike. Dignified, punctilious and energetic, James remained in office until his retirement in 1906. He died three years later.

THE PRECISE location of the University Registry was a matter which provoked keen debate and some quite remarkable displays of parochial rivalry, malice and jealousy. At least ten towns claimed to be in the running for the honour and the race occasioned much jostling and in-fighting (*Plate 16*). The favourite, Cardiff, based its case on its position as the hub of the commercial life of Wales, while Swansea, deeply resentful of Cardiff's 'grasping spirit', put up an ambitious and lavishly funded scheme which won the fervent support of O. M. Edwards. Mindful of the dangers of permitting the public to identify the University of Wales with the University College of South Wales and Monmouthshire, Aberystwyth extolled its merits as the 'mother college', while Caernarfon stressed its historic role and thoroughgoing Welshness. Several other towns, including Llandrindod, Newport, Tywyn, Wrexham and Welshpool, submitted elaborate printed applications and members of the University Court listened gravely to the impassioned and sometimes amusing speeches of their delegates. 'The Battle of the Sites' raged so furiously that the *South Wales Daily News* was moved to quote Kipling: 'The cities are full of pride, murmuring each to each.' Appalled by the whole business, the editor of Cardiff's student magazine declared: 'We propose to put our money upon Puffin Isle!' In the event, the Court funked the issue. In 1897, by a majority of four to one, it was decided to house the Registrar and his staff temporarily in 'neutral' Brecon and to postpone a final decision for five years. Candidates who had embarked on fruitless errands to the Court were much aggrieved and, as one cynic remarked, the authorities had arrived at 'a thoroughly Welsh conclusion'.

16

Burning jealousies over the location of the headquarters of the University cooled considerably after 1897 and the size, wealth and range of facilities of Cardiff increasingly made it a clear favourite. Cardiff's claims were regularly pressed by the *Western Mail* and the *South Wales Daily News*, the two most influential daily newspapers in Wales, but what eventually tilted the balance in its favour was the generous offer of £6,000 by the city Corporation towards the building of a permanent registry in Cathays Park. On 13 November 1903 the foundation-stone of the Registry of the University of Wales was laid by Sir Isambard Owen. Irreverent students cried 'Are you a mason?' and 'Mind your toes', and Edward Thomas (Cochfarf) delighted the crowds not only by speaking in Welsh but also by claiming that the memorial stone was a symbol of national unity in Wales. Following the ceremony, 230 dignitaries were ferried to the Town Hall for a sumptuous luncheon. The Registry building was opened in 1904 (*Plate 17*) and its staff has shouldered administrative burdens and complemented the work of each separate College registry ever since.

17

The University Seal (*Plate 18*) was designed by the distinguished Welsh artist Sir Edward Burne-Jones (1833–98). The obverse of the Seal reveals an instructor sitting under an arcade and holding an open book. He represents Wisdom and Knowledge. He is flanked by two standing figures, representing either students or graduates of the University, holding books. The shields of the three constituent Colleges, with their devices of the Rose, the Castle and the Mace, also appear. The legend surrounding the seal is taken from the Vulgate Latin version of Isaiah 58.10 and 12 ('Then shall thy light rise in obscurity, and they that shall be of thee shall build the old waste places'). Below the seated figure is the Welsh motto of the University – *Goreu Awen Gwirionedd* (The Best Inspiration is Truth). The reverse side of the Seal exhibits a building, representing the University, located between the mountains and the sea. The legend is drawn from Lucretius, Book 11, line 8: 'Edita doctrina sapientum templa serena.' University Statutes require that the Common Seal be secured with two locks. One key is held by the Registrar and a representative of the Court, and the second is held by the Chancellor and his Deputy.

University of Wales—Prifysgol Cymru.

Seal designed by Sir Edward Burne-Jones, Bart.

18

THE ARMS and Crest of the University of Wales were granted on 2 May 1910 (*Plate 19*). The lamps signify the three original constituent Colleges, and the eight mullets or stars represent the various constituent elements of the University Court. The legend below the Shield – Scientia Ingenium Artes – encompasses the qualities of the ideal student and three of the principal areas of University study (Science, Engineering and Arts).

19

BEFORE the First World War, University graduation or 'capping' day was held in turn in each of the three constituent Colleges. The first graduate of the University of Wales was Maria Dawson (Plate 20), who gained a B.Sc. in 1896 and who, to warm applause, was 'capped' at Cardiff a year later. She also, together with Dr J. T. Jenkins, became the first Doctor of Science of the University of Wales in 1900. In the first degree ceremony in 1897 the new graduates, according to Professor J. Young Evans, 'managed their exits and entrances as if to the manner born, not a few displaying a profundity of salaaming which would have done credit to diplomatists at Yildiz Kiosk'. Subsequent graduation ceremonies, however, became a mixture of stately ritual and youthful impudence. Students passed the time in the gallery singing raucous songs and deploying pea-shooters, paper boats and confetti to telling effect. Blushing graduates were enjoined to keep time as they marched to the stage, and whenever two girls accompanied a man students began singing 'Why can't one man have two wives?' Graduates in theology were greeted with 'Hooray for the sky-pilots' and even the upright Isambard Owen trembled at the knees whenever ladies' hockey captains were urged to 'shoot! shoot!' Such was the din on occasions that it was virtually impossible for the rest of the congregation to follow the proceedings. There was uproar at the degree ceremony conducted in the Coliseum at Aberystwyth in November 1907. Students had decided to wreak vengeance on Principal T. F. Roberts for prohibiting card-playing in common rooms. The student choir was drowned by staccato cries of 'Three Blind Mice', members of the Court were showered with peas and confetti, and an enormous leek fell at the feet of Sir Isambard Owen. 'Chuck the Principal out', cried the students and Sir Isambard swiftly dissolved the ceremony and took refuge in the College. Two years later degree day at Cardiff broke up in uproar as students blew trumpets, tossed flour bags, and sang 'Sosban Fach' and 'The Wallaby War Song'. Sir T. Marchant Williams, no stranger to scenes of disorder, was moved to suggest that unless the University authorities could maintain order the ceremony of conferring of degrees might find a more suitable home at Merthyr Police Court!

20

SINCE THE first Honorary Degree Congregation in 1896, the University of Wales has honoured over 900 men and women. Among them in the pre-1914 era was the 'Welsh Wizard', David Lloyd George (*Plate 21*), who was made an honorary Ll.D. in November 1908, shortly after his appointment as Chancellor of the Exchequer. The oration prior to the capping was delivered by John Morris-Jones, Professor of Welsh at Bangor. In a fulsome paean, he quoted lines from the work of the poet Goronwy Owen: 'Rightful lord of the land of Wales, auspicious leader of our hosts, eminent in all the land of Britain, and chief of beautiful Wales.' Although such an honour was bound to come the way of a 'cottage-bred' boy who had passed to such a high office of State, Lloyd George himself was not much interested in University affairs. Whether he counted his 'capping' akin to the baubles which he later dispensed during his Premiership we cannot tell, but he is known subsequently to have declared that in order to reorganize the University of Wales properly 'the first thing would be to hire somebody to anaesthetise the three Principals!'

21

22

An Inspiration of Genius.

DAME WALES: Well, indeed, now, Marchant, bachen, whateffer are you doing?
MARCHANT: I'm drorring the likeness of our University.

23

IT WOULD be foolish to pretend that the federal structure and the constitution of the University did not attract criticism in the pre-Haldane Commission era. One of the most colourful, cantankerous and fearless figures in the University Court was Sir T. Marchant Williams (*Plate 22*), a coalminer's son who was stipendiary magistrate at Merthyr Tydfil. The founder and editor of *The Nationalist*, he was an inveterate self-publicist with an unrivalled flair for making enemies. He never enjoyed easy relations with members of the University Court and Gilbert Norwood, Professor of Greek at Cardiff, once observed of him that he 'could not bear to be agreed with by the wrong people'. His mischievous and sometimes deliberately disruptive 'tea-cup storms' in the Court attracted much attention in the press, never more so than when he launched a hard-hitting attack on Sir Isambard Owen, the Senior Deputy Chancellor who, in 1904, had been appointed Principal of Armstrong College, Newcastle-upon-Tyne. Williams expressed his dissatisfaction in no uncertain terms. He insisted that the senior Court official should be a working head resident in Wales, and that it was a 'national humiliation' to permit the unsalaried acting head of the University of Wales to serve as Principal of a 'second-rate college' in England. When Williams was once asked, 'Where is your university?', he replied: 'The trunk is at Cardiff, the feet are at Bangor, the grasping arms are at Aberystwyth, and the head is in the private room of a doctor in Newcastle-on-Tyne!' (*Plate 23*).

WE MUST now turn to life at the three original constituent Colleges. The foundation and survival of the 'College by the Sea' at Aberystwyth is a stirring tale of fortitude and sacrifice. Led by Hugh Owen, a determined band of patriots had embarked on a long and arduous struggle in the late 1850s to construct a national educational edifice. In 1867 the Castle Hotel (a failed business venture) at Aberystwyth was acquired for £10,000, and energetic fund-raising campaigns enabled the 'people's university' to open its doors five years later. Starved of funds and resources, however, the struggle to convert 'the Biarritz of Wales' into a new Athens was seemingly futile. But the College and its authorities simply refused to lie down and die. Thanks to the Herculean efforts of Hugh Owen (who was knighted in 1880), the pennies of the poor poured in. Even the calamitous fire which broke out in the chemistry laboratory in July 1885 did not dampen the proverbial 'Aber Spirit'. Under the shrewd and determined leadership of Principal Thomas Charles Edwards, the College rose like a phoenix from the ashes. People from all walks of life gave sums of money to help rebuild and maintain the curious Gothic building which, with its impressive ensemble of towers, turrets and chimneys, had won a secure place in the affections of the nation (*Plate 24*). In 1889 the College secured a government grant and a charter, thereby ensuring its future. The heroic fortitude which had sustained this fledgeling College duly passed into Welsh folk history.

24

THE UNIVERSITY College of South Wales and Monmouthshire had opened its doors for the first time on a wet and dismal Wednesday in October 1883. A total of 109 male and forty-two female students found themselves housed in ramshackle buildings. Since the College had no buildings it could call its own, the Old Infirmary Buildings in Newport Road were rented for £400 per annum (*Plate 25*). Disgruntled students discovered that their lecture rooms and laboratories were akin to refrigerators in the winter and ovens in the summer. Such inadequate premises hardly befitted the largest and richest town in Wales and cynical students derided regular promises that a new and handsome home was in the offing:

The New Buildings are coming.
The Millennium is coming.
They are expected to arrive about the same time.

None the less, they never lost faith in the high ideals of Principal Viriamu Jones and dutifully supported the scholarly and institutional goals which he had set.

25

IN SPITE of widespread misgivings about the influence of the cathedral (the poet Caledfryn once described Bangor as 'a nest of bats and owls'), the quality of the water supply, and fears that locating a college in north-west Wales would render the Welsh 'more Welshy', the special claims of the city of Bangor as a fit and proper home for a University College had been acknowledged in 1883. The College was located in an old-fashioned hostelry called the Penrhyn Arms (*Plate 26*), which was secured on a 21-year lease from a reluctant Lord Penrhyn. When it opened its doors on 18 October 1884, thousands of well-wishers joined the invited dignitaries in a triumphant procession through the town. Professor Edward Edwards, a former student, fondly recalled tossing his cap and umbrella into the air as the participants marched by. Above the main entrance to the old hostelry were emblazoned the words 'Knowledge is Power'. It soon became clear, however, that such a small, makeshift building was unsuitable. By 1894 irate students claimed: 'our present abode, in addition to being far too small, is ugly to a degree, though . . . it is not so monstrously hideous as it is depicted in the covers of Mr O. M. Edwards' magazines, *Cymru* and *Wales*!'

26

FROM ITS inception the University of Wales was a people's university and it owed much to the selfless support of the farmers of Cardiganshire, the quarrymen of Caernarfonshire, and the miners of the Rhondda. But none of the colleges could have survived simply on the pennies and shillings of the poor. Government grants, however inadequate, were essential. So too was the financial support of public-spirited benefactors. Although industrialists and landowners were much less generous than one might have expected, there were shining exceptions. One of the founding fathers of the college at Bangor was William Rathbone (*Plate 27*), an affluent Liverpool merchant and shipowner who was MP for Caernarfonshire 1880–5 and President of the College 1892–1900. The shrewdest of businessmen, Rathbone was not only a generous benefactor but also a master of the art of wheedling funds from the thrifty and the recalcitrant. Aberystwyth, too, had good cause to be thankful for the munificence of Stuart Rendel who, following his elevation to the peerage in 1894, was elected second President of the College (1895–1913) (*Plate 28*). Lord Rendel took up the burden of assisting the College not only in order to promote his vision of 'Mid-Wales' but also from an acute sense of *noblesse oblige*. Though suspicious of Principal T. F. Roberts's grandiose building programmes, he bought land for the College and donated sums of money to augment the wretched salaries of the non-professorial staff. The Rendel Chair of English Language and Literature and a student hall of residence at Aberystwyth bear his name today. Since Cardiff was the coal metropolis of south Wales

27

and could boast a population of 164,333 by 1901, the College authorities might well have expected substantial private benefactions from coalowners, ship-brokers, merchants and bankers. The moguls of Cardiff, however, were reluctant to dig deeply into their pockets and it was left to William James Thomas of Ynys-hir (later Sir William) (*Plate 29*) to lead the way by donating the princely sum of £100,000 towards the setting up of a medical school in Cardiff.

28

29

LIMITED financial resources seriously curtailed scientific research in the three Colleges. Although Lord Kelvin, who opened the new physics and chemistry laboratories in the old Penrhyn Arms at Bangor in 1885, was impressed by the relative sophistication of the equipment, both J. J. Dobbie and Andrew Gray, each of whom was a Fellow of the Royal Society, had little scope for striking initiatives in such makeshift and overcrowded circumstances (*Plate 30*). At Cardiff, too, rudimentary scientific research was pursued by jostling students in a motley collection of sheds and attics described by T. E. Ellis as 'rabbit hutches' (*Plates 31–2*). In his inaugural address in 1919 Principal A. H. Trow must have been wearing rose-tinted spectacles when he recalled 'with a glow of satisfaction the long hours of joyous and unremunerated labour spent in research in the garrets and cellars of the old premises in Newport Road'. Students preferred to recall the stifling effects of dozens of incandescent burners on the atmosphere of the tiny laboratories. At Aberystwyth during the 1890s one small laboratory housed students in botany, zoology and geology, and, as H. J. Fleure confessed, 'research was almost

31

beyond the horizon'. At times, however, the eccentricity of some scientists and the pranks of high-spirited students helped to relieve the gloom. When D. Morgan Lewis, Professor of Physics (1891–1919), attempted to deliver a promised lecture on the science of sound, he was greeted with a deafening cacophony of sounds emitted by bugles, trombones, trumpets, penny-whistles and rubber motor-horns.

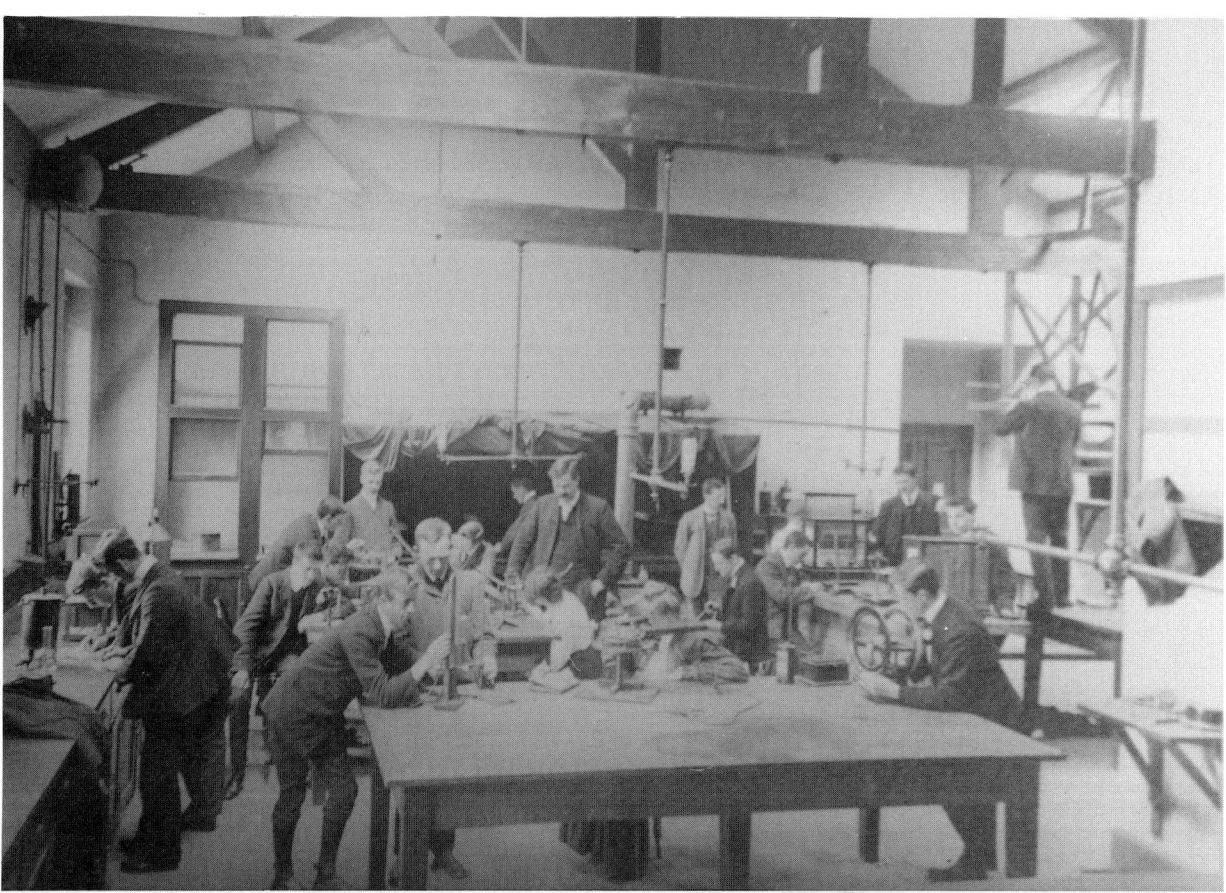

30

THE UNTIMELY death of Principal Viriamu Jones in 1901 was a tragic blow for the College at Cardiff. Shortly before his death, however, Principal Jones exhibited all his magical powers of persuasion in his last public act on behalf of the College. He appeared before members of the Council of the County Borough of Cardiff and swept them off their feet with a stirring speech in which he voiced his ambitions for the College and the town which he so deeply cherished. As a result, the Corporation donated ten acres of land in Cathays Park as a free gift to the College. A public appeal for a building fund had already been launched in 1895 and by 1903–4 receipts totalled nearly £50,000. The College was thus emboldened to invite four distinguished architects to submit plans for a new building. The winner of the competition was William Douglas Caröe (pictured in *Plate 33* in middle-age), a Liverpool-born architect who had been educated at Ruabon Grammar School. Although a marvellously inventive and progressive architect, Caröe was a fastidious, gruff and sometimes cantankerous man. He took cold baths each morning until he was well over the age of seventy, and it was perhaps appropriate that he inspired chilly awe in his colleagues and servants. He is reputed to have once ordered a shabby workman to remove himself from a scaffold.

33

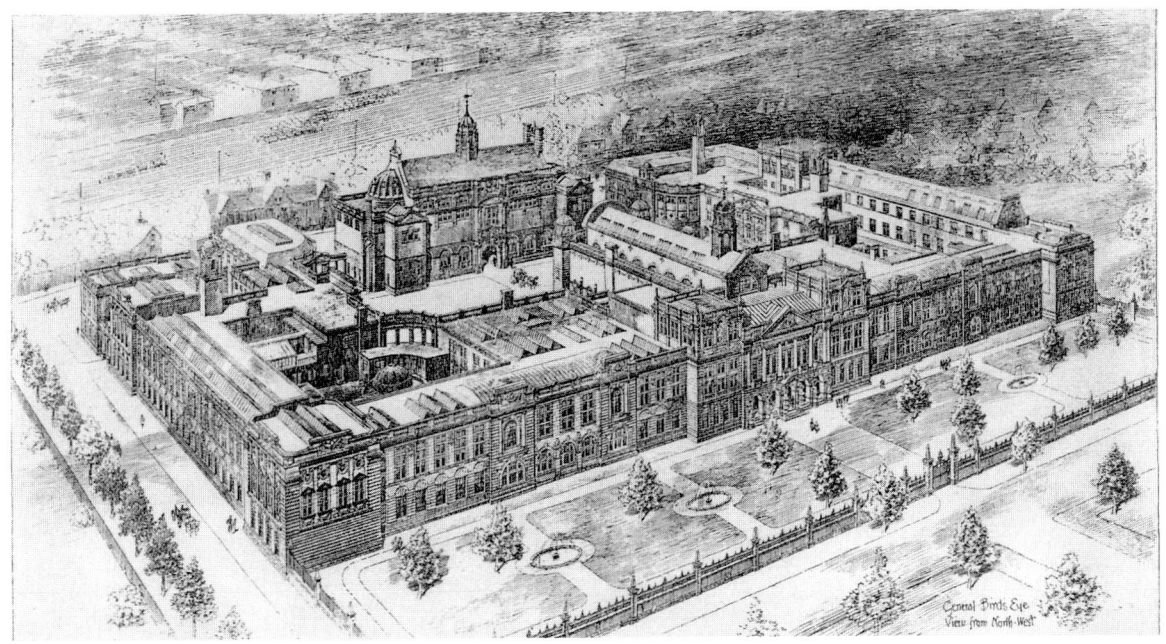

34

THE COLLEGE authorities were deeply impressed by the ingenuity and thoroughness of Carôe's plans (some of which are reproduced in *Plates 34–5*), which were chiefly inspired by the silent dignity and charm of the ancient seats of learning at Oxford and Cambridge. As he put it: 'I have in mind the delightful classical and semi-classical examples in both our ancient universities, and have endeavoured to give a flavour to the building which, while being distinctively modern and of its time, is intended to recall some of the feeling which is so characteristic of that typically British, and at the same time scholarly, architectural development. A monumental symmetry has been in the main preserved but not slavishly.' Carôe's celebrated bird's eye view from 'a flying machine' envisaged a Great Hall completing the quadrangle of the Great Court, but his hopes in this direction were never fulfilled. It is to the discredit of the University of Wales that the brilliantly gifted Carôe, who died in Cyprus in 1938, was never awarded an honorary degree.

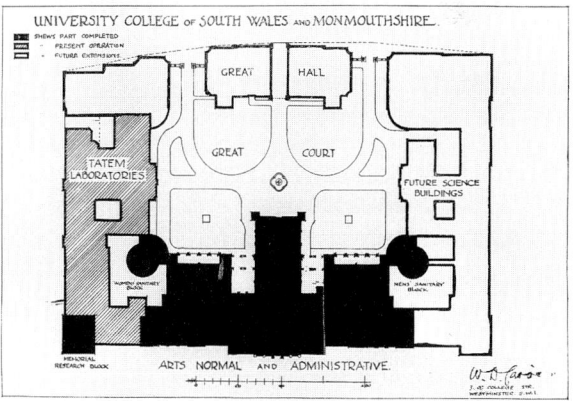

35

THE STREETS of Cardiff, decorated with flags, festoons and bunting, were crowded on 28 June 1905 when the Prince of Wales, in his capacity as Chancellor of the University, paid his first visit to Cardiff to lay the foundation stone of the new College buildings in Cathays Park (*Plate 36*). A grandstand large enough to accommodate 2,000 guests had been erected, and before it stood a raised dais under a canopy, flanked by platforms for the royal party. When the Prince, escorted by the Glamorgan Imperial Yeomanry, arrived, he was greeted by the National Anthem, 'For He's a Jolly Good Fellow' (a spontaneous contribution by some 600 students) and 'God Bless the Prince of Wales'. Following the Prince's speech, in which, according to the excited correspondent of the *Western Mail*, 'there was a ring of manliness and statesmanship in every sentence uttered', the architect W. D. Caröe presented him with a specially designed trowel and mallet. To loud cheers, the foundation stone was lowered into place.

36

In October 1909 the handsome new College buildings at Cardiff were opened by the Earl of Plymouth, President of the College (*Plate 37*). It was not widely appreciated at the time, however, that the financial situation was parlous. As 'Dame Cardiff' bewailed the plight of the College in J. M. Staniforth's cartoon (*Plate 38*), frantic efforts were being made to persuade affluent businessmen to make financial pledges. The total cost of the new building had been estimated at around £290,000, but by the end of June 1910 contributions to the appeal fund had only reached £78,000. As the historian of the College, S. B. Chrimes laconically noted, the new college was built 'not indeed on sand, but on a pile of debt (equal to about four times the then annual general income)'. It was of some comfort, however, that as a result of the recommendations of the Raleigh Report in 1909 the Treasury agreed to increase its grant for university education in Wales from £16,000 to £31,000, of which Cardiff received the largest sum of £9,500. Aberystwyth and Bangor each received annual grants of £8,000, while £5,500 was set aside for the central organization.

A Local Laocoon.

Dame Cardiff: Dear me! What an uncomfortable position to be in! I feel very sorry for them.

38

Town and Gown; or Moving into their new Home.

37

31

On 9 July 1907 King Edward VII visited Bangor to lay the foundation stone, inscribed in Welsh and Latin, of a new Arts Building (*Plate 39*). Five years earlier the College had set up a Permanent Buildings Fund, with Lewis D. Jones (Llew Tegid) as secretary, and had launched a vigorous fund-raising campaign. Once the Corporation of Bangor had presented a new ten-acre site at Penrallt to the College in August 1903, no avenues for raising substantial sums of money remained unexplored. Once more, quarrymen were not found wanting, and some farmers even offered animals in lieu of cash. Children in local schools sacrificed pennyworths of sweets in order to swell the coffers of the College. Within ten years, nearly £100,000 had been collected. The visit of the King in 1907 was a joyous occasion, all the more so when a richly deserved knighthood was conferred upon Principal Reichel during the ceremonies. A steady drizzle in the early morning had ceased the moment the royal party arrived, and some onlookers swore to their dying day that a shaft of sunlight shot across the foundation stone as the King tapped it with his mallet.

39

WORK ON the new buildings at Bangor began immediately after the ceremony in 1907. Indeed, the event had been so splendidly organized that an appreciable number of subscriptions came to hand from benefactors and well-wishers during the summer. The King himself promised a hundred guineas though, much to the chagrin and embarrassment of the College authorities, not a single royal penny ever found its way to Bangor. Here we see the local work-force, with their masters, suitably hatted and, in some cases, perching precariously on scaffolds (*Plate 40*). Plans had been designed by the architect Henry Thomas Hare, though it should be pointed out that no less a person than the apparently omniscient Sir Isambard Owen (who had been appropriately named after the engineer Isambard Brunel!) had pointed out flaws in Hare's initial plans and suggested that the architect should adapt the building to the splendid site on the Upper Bangor ridge rather than *vice versa*. Hare happily concurred and ensured that his noble building took full advantage of the sloping hillside.

40

THE NEW buildings at Bangor, which cost £106,000, were opened by King George V on 14 July 1911. The King was deeply impressed by the serene dignity of a building which was described in the periodical *Wales* as 'the finest architectural pile in the Principality' (*Plate 41*). The genius of the architect drew many admiring comments and no message was more apt than the sentiments expressed by Henry Jones, former Professor of Philosophy at Bangor and now Professor of Philosophy at the University of Glasgow: 'What better can I wish for the College than that its inner soul may be as beautiful as its outer shell.' The new building comprised lecture and administrative rooms, common rooms, halls, kitchens, a splendid library wing built by the Worshipful Company of Drapers, and a Great Hall erected through the generosity of Sir John Prichard-Jones, Vice-President of the College. During the ceremonies on 'the Glorious Fourteenth', knighthoods were conferred upon Sir Henry Lewis, Sir Edward Anwyl and Sir William Goscombe John, and at the lavish garden party which followed members of the College's Officers' Training Corps consumed most of the cakes and tea. On such a warm and memorable day, even po-faced Principal Reichel felt able to smile broadly with satisfaction.

41

TO SURVIVE and prosper, universities need not only costly and sophisticated buildings but also scholars for whom teaching and research is an invigorating labour of love. When the University College of Wales, Aberystwyth, embarked on its twenty-second session in 1893–4 it could boast twenty-four members of teaching staff. Its new Principal, Thomas Francis Roberts (1891–1919), was a classical scholar of high esteem who, throughout his principalship, maintained a New Testament Greek class for students. His staff, scandalously paid and grossly overburdened with teaching duties, were on the whole competent rather than inspiring, but it was no doubt of comfort to them that Aberystwyth was, in the words of O. M. Edwards, 'a gentle place to live, a cheap place, a healthy place'. At least two brilliant scholars, however, made a lasting impression on their students. Dr Hermann Ethé (*Plate 42*, seated, extreme right), a true polymath, not only taught Italian, German, French, Spanish, Hebrew, Arabic, Syriac and Sanskrit but advertised in the College Calendar his readiness 'to read with students in other Oriental Languages'. Charles Harold Herford (*Plate 42*, second row, extreme right) Professor of English Literature since 1887, was also an inspiring and stimulating teacher who, in 1901, was appointed to the Chair of English Literature in the Victoria University of Manchester. Both scholars would have heartily endorsed their Principal's favourite maxim: 'Not Wales for the Welsh but Wales for the world.'

42

IN SPITE of the dilapidated and dispiriting buildings in which the College at Cardiff was housed in the late Victorian period, Principal J. Viriamu Jones recruited uncommonly gifted scholars to strengthen the academic structure of the College and to serve the particular needs of the people of south Wales. One appreciative student described him as 'the Atlas upon whose shoulders the two hemispheres of University business, administrative and academical, have rested from the beginning'. His principalship was a fruitful one, and by 1896 there were twenty departments in the College. Engineering ('with heaven knows how many chimneys', claimed the student magazine), mining education, metallurgy and physiology were given high priority even though laboratories were wretchedly cramped and poorly equipped. Among the most distinguished members of staff in *Plate 43*, a photograph taken in 1893, are the musician Dr Joseph Parry (standing, fifth from left), the botanist (later Principal) A. H. Trow (standing, fourth from right), the French scholar Paul Barbier (standing, extreme right), and Thomas Powel, Professor of Celtic (seated, third from right). Principal Viriamu Jones seems momentarily distracted by the presence of a member of the Education Department.

43

I F IT BE true that the best teachers are more than a little eccentric, then Aberystwyth in its early years was bounteously blessed. The most celebrated figure on the staff was Dr Hermann Ethé (*Plate 44*), a brilliant and many-sided linguist who served the College with unswerving devotion for nearly forty years. In the view of R. T. Jenkins, who sat at Ethé's feet, the most apposite description of this man of genius was 'stupendous'. His thunderous voice echoed through classrooms and corridors, and his booming laugh was likened to 'the sound of a marble in the depths of a barrel'. Ethé's love of alcohol, good food and cigars made him a distinctive figure in a community where the spirit of temperance and abstinence was very much alive. At one of Principal T. F. Roberts's insufferably abstemious parties, Ethé was invited by a waitress to select either lemonade or water. 'Ach!', he bellowed, 'Vod does id madder vich?' The manner of his departure from Aberystwyth brought lasting disgrace to the community. During the Great War, Ethé found himself the innocent victim of the clash of arms. Bilious Methodists and xenophobic local councillors organized noisy anti-German demonstrations outside Ethé's home and at the College. In spite of the courageous efforts of Principal T. F. Roberts to pacify the mob, the German scholar, as the contrite editor of *The Dragon* put it, was 'hounded from the town, while fisherwomen yelled, school-children huzzaed, and notable councillors made orations'. Heartbroken, Ethé died in Reading in June 1917.

44

ONE OF THE most exceptionally gifted teachers at Bangor was James Johnston Dobbie, Professor of Chemistry and Geology (1885–1903) (*Plate 45*). This many-sided Scotsman possessed an unusual talent for communicating science both to students and laymen. His extra-mural lectures on agricultural chemistry kindled keen interest in agricultural education among small farmers in north Wales and it was as a result of his initiative that the Department of Agriculture was established in 1888. 'In many a lonely farmhouse, where the old tongue is still the language of the hearth', wrote W. Rhys Roberts in a most florid appreciation of his colleague, 'the College-trained son explains to his father, in connexion with Dr Dobbie's name, the advantages of the scientific cultivation of the soil; and though the old-time farmer may be slow to believe that science is the true philanthropist that can make two blades of grass grow where but one grew before, yet surely though slowly knowledge wins its way and ignorance is baffled and retreats.' In 1903 Dobbie was appointed Director of the National Museum of Scotland.

45

46

The Bubble.

47

NO HISTORIAN stood higher in the esteem of his contemporaries than John Edward Lloyd, Professor of History at Bangor (1899–1930) (*Plate 46*), whose magisterial two-volumed work *A History of Wales from the Earliest Times to the Edwardian Conquest* (1911) was researched and written when he was not only a Lecturer in Welsh History at Bangor but also Secretary and Registrar of the College. Although his Olympian manner could freeze conversations and overawe strangers, he could be whimsical and engaging in private. He used to refer self-deprecatingly to his researches as 'pottering' and claimed that his daily routine was to act as 'lecturer in the morning, registrar in the afternoon, and researcher in the evening'. Of his passion for history there was no doubt and Saunders Lewis properly described him as 'the lamplighter of the lost centuries'. As the cartoon in the student publication *The Undertaker* reveals (*Plate 47*), Lloyd was bitterly disappointed that a knighthood was not conferred upon him on the occasion of the opening of the new College buildings in 1911. Indeed, that honour was unforgivably delayed until 1934, by which time Lloyd had retired. On the occasion of his death in 1947, R. T. Jenkins recalled 'the dignified presence, the resonant voice, the stately diction' of a man whose works have not only enlightened his fellow countrymen but also lightened the labours of his successors.

BANGOR could also boast pioneers in the history of aviation. The researches of George Hartley Bryan FRS, a brilliant, eccentric (and often inebriated) mathematician (he was Professor from 1896 to 1926) engaged the interest of outside experts on aeronautics. In 1910 he and his co-worker, William Ellis Williams (seen in the cockpit in *Plate 48*) constructed a curious monoplane made largely from ash and bamboo. It was dubbed 'The Bamboo Bird'. Bryan's theory of the control and stability of aircraft earned him the much coveted Gold Medal of the Royal Aeronautical Society in 1915.

48

FROM 1888 until his death in 1903 the Head of Music at Cardiff was 'the Great Doctor', Joseph Parry (*Plate 49*), a former pit-boy and ironworker who became a professional musician and the composer of the first Welsh opera *Blodwen* (1878) as well as countless hymns, cantatas, choruses and oratorios. Parry was a highly stimulating, if unconventional teacher, and one tale of his experiences in the classroom during his earlier career as the first Professor of Music at Aberystwyth has passed into folk memory. 'In 1879 Parry was one day standing before the blackboard giving the class a lesson. Principal T. C. Edwards was present, evidently by arrangement. Parry chalked a crotchet on the board, and called upon a student, who during the summer vacation worked in a slate quarry, to give the note its proper name. Immediately came the answer: "a *crochet*, sir". Then Parry put a 'natural' sign on the board, with a similar request to the same student. Without hesitation the reply came "a *general*, sir". By this time the Principal had got behind the blackboard, overwhelmed with the comedy of the scene.' Idolized by students and choral singers all over Wales, Parry himself remained modest about his worth and never lost the habit of referring to himself as 'a little boy from Merthyr'. By the time of his death, one obituarist described him as 'without doubt the most well-known Welshman in the world'.

49

ONE OF Viriamu Jones's earliest and most able recruits was Paul Barbier (*Plate 50*). Appointed in 1883 (and elevated to the Chair in 1904), this genial and cultivated son of a Protestant pastor from France served as Head of French for thirty-seven years. Much revered by his pupils, not least among Barbier's merits was his conviction that teaching French through the medium of Welsh was advantageous because of the close affinity between the two languages. In 1910, however, his negligence brought the University of Wales into grave disrepute. Examination papers in French had in error been leaked to students and, as a result, 350 irate students were summoned to re-sit examinations which were rather more demanding than the original versions. The stormy petrel of University life, Sir T. Marchant Williams immediately seized upon a golden opportunity to embarrass the University authorities. In a series of intemperate letters to the *Western Mail*, he declared that the University was 'on the rocks'. He accused professors over a wide range of disciplines of conveying the essence of examination papers to their students either directly in the classroom or in casual conversation. Williams did not believe that internal examiners could be trusted and Barbier's gaffe (an inquiry absolved him of deliberate intent) prompted the University to reassess the system.

50

THE NUMBER of students at the three Welsh Colleges at the turn of the nineteenth century was, by modern standards, extremely small. Although the number of students at Bangor had increased from fifty-eight in 1884–5 to 277 (180 males and ninety-seven females) in 1900–1, it was still possible for John Wickens of the Retina Studios, Bangor, to capture the bulk of the student body in this photograph taken in 1901 (*Plate 51*). J. E. Lloyd once proudly (though not entirely correctly) declared that 'we claim the whole of North Wales as our parish'. In fact, the overwhelming majority of Bangor's students hailed from Anglesey and Caernarfonshire. In 1900–1 only thirty-three came from south Wales. In contrast, in the same session the student population at Aberystwyth was not only larger but also more cosmopolitan. Of 476 students (260 males, and 216 females), it is true that most were natives of Cardiganshire, Carmarthenshire and Glamorgan, but there were also 160 students from England and a sprinkling of visitors from Scotland, Ireland, Germany, Spain and India. One student sensed that Aberystwyth was permeated with 'a healthy enthusiasm, in which the Celtic fire is tempered by the cooler but less uncertain conservatism of the Anglo-Saxon'! Cardiff sported the largest student body in 1900–1, but its catchment area was every bit as parochial as that of Bangor. Its complement of 628 students (366 males and 262 females) included 194 from Cardiff itself, 256 from other parts of Glamorgan, sixty-six from Monmouthshire, forty-two from England and abroad, and only ten from north Wales. This may account for the following observation made by a Cardiff fresher in 1901: 'I can think of no institution where so thorough an *esprit de corps* obtains.'

51

Although prejudice against women and in particular regarding their intellectual prowess lingered on in ultra-conservative circles, the University of Wales could legitimately boast of being 'in the van of progress'. The University of Wales Charter of 1893 granted women full educational equality with men. Both Cardiff and Bangor had opened their doors to women from the outset and a shamefaced Aberystwyth followed suit in 1884. Women students were required to fill in a certificate and forward it to the Lady Principal prior to the commencement of the academic session (*Plate 52*). When this photograph of women students at Aberystwyth was taken *c.*1895 (*Plate 53*), 135 women students were enrolled in the College, but by 1908–9 they had outstripped men in numbers (218 women, 212 men). Such women chafed under a host of petty and childish rules and regulations which were designed to keep the sexes as far apart as possible. When, in November 1898, a male student at Aberystwyth was rusticated for two terms for conducting a conversation with a female student through an open window of Alexandra Hall, the *Western Mail* gleefully plied its readers with details of the 'Romeo and Juliet' episode and a noisy, almost riotous, student demonstration threw the College Senate into utter confusion. Three years later students at Bangor went on a week-long strike when two males paid the price for dallying with females following the College Eisteddfod. The two male culprits were rusticated for the remainder of the Lent term and the two females were confined to barracks from five onwards each evening. Members of Senate became even more apoplectic when it was reported that two students had been seen hand-in-hand in the distant parish of Llansadwrn in Anglesey! Bangor's Romeo and Juliet were duly expelled and when pleas for a stay of execution were ignored the student body, by a small majority, decided to call off the strike.

52

53

EVER SINCE its foundation in 1883 Cardiff had led the way in admitting women students on equal terms with men, and two years later a house was secured in Richmond Road to house a small number of them. On 8 October 1895, a spacious new hall of residence, called Aberdare Hall (*Plate 54*), and located on the outskirts of the city, was opened by Mrs E. M. Sidgwick of Newnham College, Cambridge. A Jacobean-style building, it owed its existence to the selfless zeal of an enthusiastic committee, headed by Lady Aberdare, to a generous loan from the College, and a grant of £2,000 from the Pfeiffer trustees. The first Lady Principal, Miss Ethel Hurlbatt, was succeeded in 1898 by her sister Kate, who won and retained the respect and affections of women students over a period of thirty-six years. Residential fees at the hall ranged from £31.10s. to £42 per annum, and the forty-three students were offered simply furnished but cosy and generally well ventilated rooms lit by electric light. This photograph of Miss Kate Hurlbatt and her students was taken during the session 1903–4 (*Plate 55*).

54

55

ASYLUM or Workhouse? Gibes of this sort were commonly voiced by irreverent male students as they walked past this grey, forbidding building located at the foot of Constitution Hill at the northern end of the Promenade in Aberystwyth (*Plate 56*). Alexandra Hall was officially opened by the Princess of Wales (after whom it was named) on 26 June 1896. A five-storey building, initially designed to house a hundred women students, Alexandra Hall was established in order to provide young women students with relatively congenial (though extremely sheltered) purpose-built residential quarters. The Lady Principal, Miss E. A. Carpenter, kept students under close surveillance. This diminutive but redoubtable woman – memorably described by Professor H. J. Fleure as 'a very mighty atom' – was the very epitome of Victorian rectitude and discipline. Her charges were expected to attend meals punctually, return to their rooms by 10 p.m. sharp (when all entrance doors were locked and bolted), and never to dally in public with male students except when a reliable chaperone was present. Olive Marsh (the future Lady Stamp), who was a student at Alexandra Hall in 1898–1900, joyfully noted in one of her letters: 'Miss Carpenter is away. There is such an air of freedom about the place.' Yet few could not bring themselves to admire the style and authority with which Miss Carpenter governed the hall, and when she retired, aged seventy, in 1905 there was a genuine feeling of sadness as well as relief.

57

O N HER ARRIVAL at Alexandra Hall in October 1898, Olive Marsh, the most detailed and lively of correspondents, informed her fiancé with delighted surprise of the privacy and comfort of her room (Plate 57). 'I made the acquaintance of my cubicle and, very soon, got into bed. It's such a dear little bed, spring mattress, very fine sheets and a nice white quilt. In my cubicle I have a chest of drawers, a washstand, a chair, a nice rug and a looking glass . . . I couldn't wish for things to be nicer . . . I am very happy here, everything is so lovely. I never dreamt of anything so nice.' The food was tolerable, and sometimes very good, and impromptu debates, soirées and 'girls only' dances helped to while away leisure hours (Plate 58). Absurd rules and regulations severely restricted contact with males, and only on rare social occasions were men and women permitted to mix freely. 'They call this a mixed College', cried Sergeant Wakeling, the College Proctor, 'but, by gad, if they catch you mixing!' Extraordinary steps were taken to restrict the mingling of sexes. Wardens, proctors and dons prowled corridors and lurked in dark alleys in order to pounce on courting couples or revellers. Inter-

58

College soccer and rugby matches were enthusiastically supported by women partly because they provided rare opportunities for communicating and flirting with active, healthy males.

THE PURITAN spirit remained stubbornly strong well into the Edwardian period and women increasingly chafed against conventions which made the University a man's world. Some of them, against all the odds, displayed great initiative in their quest for emancipation. This cartoon (*Plate 59*), which appeared in the *Morning Leader* on 7 July 1905, suggests that points of contact between professors and lady students at Bangor were not as formal as Principal Reichel might have expected or wished. Durable alliances were clearly forged and, by an exquisite irony, the woman student who had been expelled in 1901 for daring to hold hands with a male student in the fastnesses of Anglesey later returned to Bangor to marry the widowed T. Witton Davies, Professor of Semitics. Whether Bangor truly deserved the sobriquet 'Cupid's College' is presumably a matter for debate.

Cartoon of the Day.

DON'T CRUSH!

[It is announced that at least six professors at Bangor University have married lady students.]

59

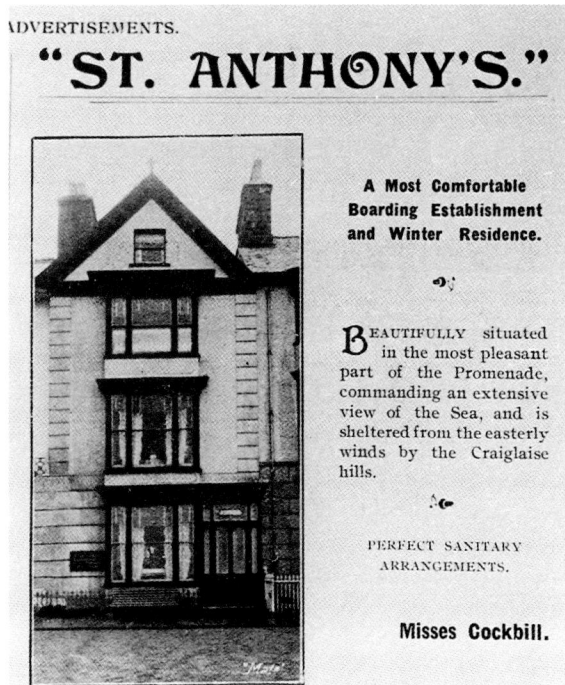

60

baths and some decidedly inferior guest houses still depended on oil lamps and wax candles. Lodging-house keepers were expected to report to the Principal any students who broke the 10 p.m. curfew or spent the night away from their lodgings (Plate 61). Draconian punishments inevitably followed. Penurious students, too, had good cause to recall frugal landladies. A correspondent in the *Cap and Gown* wrote ruefully: 'DIGS – A euphemism for a place where you are a stranger and they take you in; may be divided into three classes – bad, worse, worst. Presiding genius – i.e. landlady – is said to keep lodgers: in reality they keep her. The original home of the "vanishing loaf" and "melting butter" tricks. Like the Pelican, the landlady has a large bill and, true to the instincts of her class, keeps pecking. Usually Digs are the Dickens, and when they are not the Dickens they are the deuce.'

61

LODGINGS – or digs as they were called – were carefully examined by College authorities before males were permitted to enter them (Plate 60). Since many landlords and landladies shared the passion for thrift, hard work and discipline which characterized the Victorian and Edwardian bourgeoisie, luxuries were rare. Few lodgings had

THE STOUTEST defenders of disciplinary codes were those martinets called Proctors or Head Porters. When Sergeant Wakeling, a rotund former soldier with a barking voice, was appointed Head Porter at Aberystwyth in 1896, students swiftly dubbed him 'the Bulldog' and informed their colleagues in sister Colleges that 'the Prinny's been and bought us a bow wow'. Wakeling cut an imposing figure in his black uniform with scarlet braiding (Plate 62), and untutored visitors to the College were apt to mistake him for the Vice-Chancellor of the University, a misapprehension which was strengthened by his opening gambit: 'Me and the Principal think . . .' (Plate 63). Wakeling spoke

62

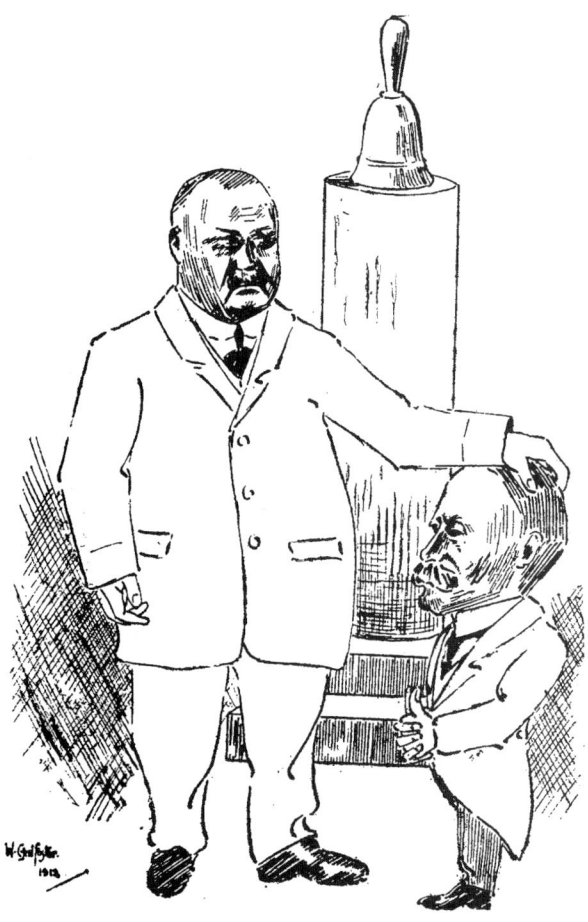

"ME AND THE PRINCIPAL."

63

with great authority on every subject under the sun and was so well informed on College matters that he confidently assured staff and students alike that the institution would disintegrate without him. Under the title 'Gems from the Janitor', students printed his *obiter dicta* and malapropisms with great relish in *The Dragon*. Among his most memorable sayings were: 'The Senate is quite right to insist upon compulsory hepidemic dress', 'Prinny receives many unanimous letters', and 'The two things are synonymous, but one is more synonymous than the other'. Although his grammatical novelties and trite sayings provoked much hilarity, woe betide those students who publicly sought to puncture his ponderous dignity. For Wakeling ruled the College Quad like a grenadier and vigorously implemented the regimen imposed on students. He was not a man to be trifled with, and when he retired in 1923 the College became a much duller place.

STUDENT life in the three colleges was busy and buoyant in the years before the First World War. A host of clubs and societies, including dramatics, music, athletics, scientific, socialist, chemistry and Celtic, offered students ample opportunity to display their gifts, sometimes presumably at the expense of their academic studies. Cardiff took the initiative in co-ordinating the activities of such societies. Its Students' Representative Council, instituted in 1896–7, comprised thirty members, who represented a myriad interests in the College. An amalgamation fee of 9s. for men and 7s. 6d. for women enabled each individual student to join any of the clubs or societies affiliated to the SRC. To some degree, the SRC was a reaction against excessively stringent College rules which, by the end of the nineteenth century, were viewed as a tiresome hindrance to full student autonomy. When Bangor and Aberystwyth established their own Councils in 1898–9 and 1900 respectively, the prospect of exercising much wider control over their own affairs was greatly relished by students:

Now at last an outward sign
Of students' fellowship is born –
The S.R.C. with powers benign
To usher in a brighter dawn.

Several of the emancipated representatives at Bangor (*Plate 64*) include the Vice-President Alice E. Smith (seated, extreme right) and the secretaries Gwladys Pritchard Williams (seated, extreme left) and Wynn P. Wheldon (back row, second left). Wheldon, according to his son Huw, 'mortgaged his father's will to go to university. He looked like a soldier among academics, and an academic among soldiers'. In 1920 he was appointed Registrar at Bangor and was knighted in 1939. The reclining figure, clutching the paw of 'Pickle', the dog, is R. Silyn Roberts, a former quarryman who won the Crown at the National Eisteddfod in 1902 for a celebrated *pryddest* on 'Trystan and Esyllt'. Miss Mary Maude, warden of the Women's Hall, gazes in rapture at Principal Reichel.

64

PUBLIC-SPEAKING was held in high esteem in student circles, and the Literary and Debating Society provided a valuable apprenticeship for gifted young students who relished the cut-and-thrust of inter-College debates. In crowded debating rooms, speakers not only competed against one another but also against almost continuous heckling, barracking and gales of laughter. According to R. T. Jenkins, 'the Lit. and Deb. was a stormy and irreverent place' at Aberystwyth largely because 'those sons of Belial who sat on the radiators at the rear of the audience made a nervous speaker's life a misery'. Clarity of thought, articulate expression, impromptu wit and repartee were greatly prized, and particularly animated jousts occurred whenever controversial issues such as 'That the aims of the Labour Party run counter to the ideals of the Welsh nation' or 'That England is on the down-grade' were debated. Among the luminaries in this Gynnadl Gymreig (Inter-College Welsh Debate) (Plate 65), held in 1913, are the President, Professor Edward Anwyl (seated, in the centre), a formidable Celtic scholar who used to suffuse his lectures with commentaries on 'the reduplicated emphatic pronoun' and 'concessive-clause-equivalents', Kate Roberts (seated, second left), a Bangor graduate who became a most distinguished novelist and short-story writer, and Griffith John Williams (seated, extreme right), a blacksmith's son who graduated at Aberystwyth and, having successfully unfathomed the tortuous mind of Iolo Morganwg, was rewarded in 1947 with the Chair of Welsh at Cardiff.

65

ALTHOUGH Welsh was introduced as a degree subject in the University of Wales in 1896 and a common syllabus adopted by the three Colleges, English remained the language of instruction in each department. Moreover, the academic and administrative affairs of the Colleges were conducted in English. Apart from Welsh societies like Y Geltaidd at Aberystwyth and Y Cymric at Bangor, Welsh-speakers kept a low profile, and even celebrations on St David's Day were heavily anglicized. 'Welshmen seem to be too shy to speak their own language', complained one disenchanted Bangor student following a conversazione at Bangor on 1 March 1903. Yet the Welsh societies, particularly by the eve of the First World War, were becoming vigorous promoters of native causes. Among the talented staff and students in Sir Edward Anwyl's final Welsh class at Aberystwyth before his death in 1914 (*Plate 66*) are T. H. Parry-Williams (extreme right in the rear), winner of the Crown and Chair at the National Eisteddfod at Wrexham in 1912, T. Gwynn Jones (middle row, second from left), the first Reader ever to be appointed by the University of Wales, and D. J. Williams (seated, second from right), a fervent Welsh nationalist who subsequently became a distinguished short-story writer.

66

STUDENTS were not slow to seize the opportunity of airing their views in College magazines. First off the starting-blocks was Aberystwyth in 1878. In spite of its unimaginative title – *The University College of Wales Magazine* – the magazine prospered for twenty-six years. When it became *The Dragon* in 1904, responsibility for its content and publication devolved to a committee of the SRC. Bangor's first venture, published in 1888, foundered after one issue only. It was revived in June 1891 and bore the prosaic title *Magazine of the University College of North Wales, Bangor*, until December 1913. It was then baptized *Mascot*. In 1928 it settled on the catch-all title *Omnibus*. Cardiff's first magazine was a distinctive piece of self-help. Made available in November 1885, it was in manuscript form. It cost less than 2s. 6d. to produce and it was placed on a table in the students' common room. Three years later a printed magazine became the norm and by 1903, appropriately christened *Cap and Gown*, it had become an acknowledged mouthpiece of student opinion (*Plate 67*). Prior to the early 1920s, little material in Welsh was published in these magazines and in 1939 the editor of *The Dragon*, vigorously defending the 'peculiarly English' tradition of the magazine, warned readers against 'that queer form of arrested mental development we know as Welsh Nationalism'.

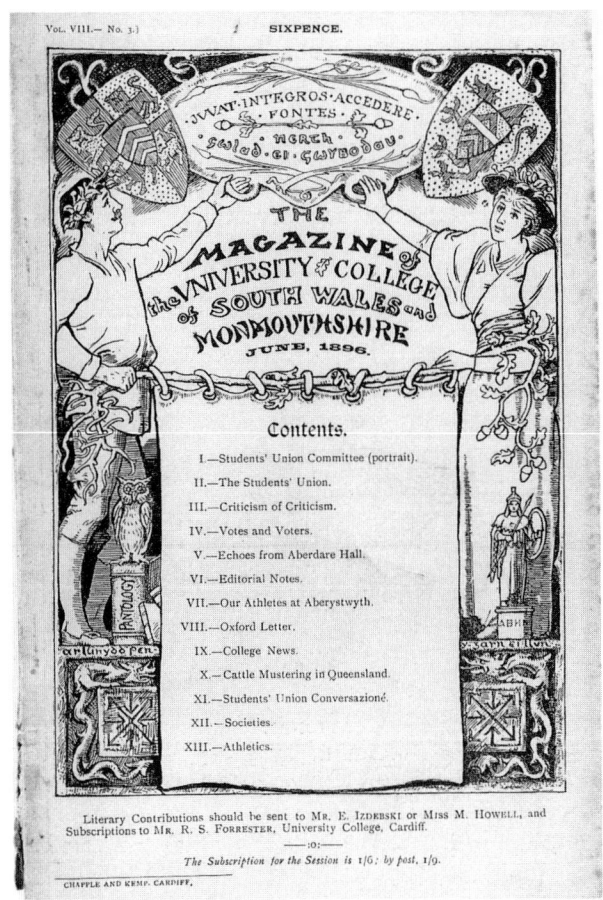

67

The extraordinary interest in music which characterized Welsh society was also mirrored in the Colleges. Choral societies flourished, partly as a consequence of the inspiring influence of Dr Joseph Parry at Aberystwyth and Cardiff. Parry believed that music ought to be a fundamental part of education and he was determined to foster musical enjoyment on a communal basis. Nor did Bangor wish to be excluded from the proliferation of musical activity. The botanist John Lloyd Williams, a lead-miner's son, was particularly keen to enable the lost tradition of Welsh folk-songs to re-enter the nation's collective memory. Williams worked closely with Llew Tegid, an accomplished eisteddfod conductor and librettist, and one of their most popular co-productions was the operetta, *Aelwyd Angharad*. In 1907 Lloyd Williams formed a small choir called 'Y Canorion' (Songsters), who specialized in folk-songs. In *Plate 68*, Lloyd Williams is the moustached figure on the extreme right and Llew Tegid the bearded figure on the extreme left. Lloyd Williams subsequently became Professor of Botany at Aberystwyth (1914–26), where he continued to pursue his musical interests with considerable zeal.

68

COLLEGE songs were often energetically declaimed whenever distinguished guests were invited. On 26 June 1912 King George V and Queen Mary visited the College at Cardiff to open the Viriamu Jones Research Laboratory (*Plate 69*). Following the ceremony they appeared on the balcony, where they were greeted and entertained by a throng of enthusiastic students. They sang two verses of the College Song, a Latin ode written by D. A. Slater, Professor of Latin, and set to music by Dr David Evans, a lecturer in music who was affectionately known as 'Dai Canary'. The Ode for Chorus and Orchestra, first performed on the occasion of the opening of the new buildings in 1909, began as follows:

69

> Confremant, confremant
> Saecula studentum,
> Quae sunt, quaeque post erunt,
> Quaeque iam fuerunt!
> Latus patet ambitus
> Nobilis Collegi;
> Nos heredes subeamus;
> Gratiarum nos agamus
> Debitum concentum.

The male students then performed the College Yell, before hurling their mortar-boards high into the air. The royal party was, by all accounts, much amused.

THE WHIRL of social activity which filled the leisure hours of staff and students alike was striking, and of gatherings 'grave and gay', wrote one sage, 'there was no end'. Among them were picnics, balls, concerts, fancy dress parties, cocoa parties, conversaziones, eisteddfodau, smokers, at-homes, debates and soirées. Soirées were known to last for up to six hours and might include songs, duets, choruses, topicals, recitations, quartets, living waxworks, tableaux vivants, comic plays, comedies, farces and parodies. This soirée, 'Spreading the News' (*Plate 70*), a one-act comedy by Lady Gregory, was performed as part of the St David's Day celebrations at Aberystwyth on 3 March 1911. Selections from J. Lloyd Williams's operetta *Aelwyd Angharad* were also sung in the same programme, together with a spirited rendering of 'Crossing the Plain' by a male voice party. One correspondent in *The Dragon* sourly (and unfairly) described soirée plays as 'forty minutes of unadulterated drivel', but audiences clearly derived considerable pleasure and amusement from such activities.

70

PLAYS, THEATRICAL events, conversaziones and soirées also helped to encourage friendly staff-student relations, although it must be said that even in the most serious productions the standard of acting often came perilously close to crossing the fine line which separated comedy from farce. At Aberystwyth, productions in the pre-First World War years were directed with autocratic precision by Professor J. W. Marshall (known to all and sundry as 'Jimmy'). Marshall not only ensured that most of the staff appeared behind the footlights but were also (to the chagrin of students) given the best parts. In the performance of Shakespeare's *Much Ado about Nothing* in December 1894, Joseph Brough, Professor of Philosophy, appeared as Benedick, Edward Anwyl, Professor of Celtic, as Friar Francis, and the incomparable Hermann Ethé as Dogberry (*Plate 71*). A bemused student correspondent subsequently wrote in the student magazine: 'We find it difficult to judge Dr Ethé's study of Dogberry. It was always entertaining and certainly memorable, but we are doubtful whether his general conception of the part was altogether Shakespearian.'

71

72

between staff and students. With characteristic self-deprecation, he once said of himself: 'I am a philosopher by training, a historian from necessity, but a jester by temperament.' Among the many parts which he played on stage was the role of Sir Lucius O'Trigger in Sheridan's *The Rivals* in 1897 (*Plate 73*). Students (particularly women) adored him, and *The Dragon* rightly described him as 'one of us'. An Aber man through and through, his association with the College extended over forty years. He died, aged sixty-eight, in 1933.

73

MEMBERS of the academic staff participated freely in the social life of the student calendar, and none in the three Colleges took a keener interest in student activities in the concert hall, theatre and sports fields than Edward Edwards, lecturer and subsequently Professor of History at Aberystwyth (1895–1930). Unlike his celebrated (but austere!) brother O. M. Edwards, 'Teddy Eddy' bubbled with waggish humour and wit (*Plate 72*). Devastatingly handsome, debonair and charming, he did much to foster amiable town-gown relations as well as close and happy co-operation

RELATIONS between staff and students, however, were not all sweetness and light. Staid and stuffy scholars and administrators were lampooned in student publications, particularly in the short-lived magazine, *The Undertaker* (1912–13), in which Bangor students indulged in raillery and ridicule calculated to cause pain. The victims in *Plate 74* are J. E. Lloyd, Professor of History (Pomposo), Principal Reichel (Largo), Edward Taylor Jones, Professor of Physics (Furioso Crescendo) and George Hartley Bryan, Professor of Pure and Applied Mathematics (Tremulo Prestissimo).

74

THE CULT of athleticism did not take long to reach the University of Wales and the 'Inter-College Week' from 1893 onwards was marked by sporting contests which both sharpened the edge of inter-College rivalries and fostered a sense of loyalty to the University as a whole (*Plate 75*). Sporting visits were often dubbed the Colleges' 'Saturnalia'. On such ceremonial occasions it was not unusual for visiting teams to be greeted by Zulu chieftains, Indian braves, pierrots on stilts, buglers, fiddlers and drummers. At Bangor, in particular, town and gown used to take to the streets to celebrate the arrival of the 'enemy', and as they emerged from the station a rousing cry of 'Hip! hip! hooray! Bravo! Bravissimo! Sss-boom dra! Sss-boom dra! Bravo! Bravissimo!' pierced the air. The horse-drawn Garth Bus, seen here in May 1906 carrying apprehensive cricketers and tennis-players from Aberystwyth at the junction of College Road with Holyhead Road (*Plate 76*), used to make its way noisily through the streets of Bangor to the Ladies' Hostel, where welcoming speeches were loudly declaimed before the visitors were escorted to their respective quarters.

Social Events.

Sat., 25th Feb. **Chair Eisteddfod.**
Parish Hall. 6 p.m.

Mon 27th Feb. Celtic Debate (Inter Coll)

Tues., 28th Feb. **Inter-Varsity Debate.**
Subject: "That Wealth and Praise are the only effective inducements to human action." Parish Hall. 6 p.m.

Wed., 1st March. **Inter-Coll. Dinner.**
Ward's Café. 6.30 p.m.

Inter-Coll. Smoker.
Men's Club. 8 p.m.

Swimming Club Dance.
Bryn-y-mor Hut. 6.30 p.m.

Thurs., 2nd M'rch. **Gymnastic Display.**
Coliseum. 7.45 p.m.

Fri., 3rd March. **Inter-Coll. Procession** to meet Swansea Rugger.

St. David's Day Soiree.
6 p.m.

Sat., 4th March. **Dance.**
Parish Hall. 7.30 p.m.

75

76

IN THE YEAR in which the University of Wales was founded, the national rugby XV won the Triple Crown, probably in celebration. Alas, the standard of rugby during that year in the 'mother' college at Aberystwyth was truly lamentable. The College XV (*Plate 77*) not only lost to St David's College, Lampeter, but could also only draw against Lampeter schoolboys. Although the students' rugby correspondent claimed that the referee in the game against the Lampeter students had displayed 'almost complete ignorance of the laws of the game', the truth is that not even the noisy presence of attractive women students could rouse the team from its torpor. Things did improve, however, and by 1909 the College team was deemed worthy of pitting its wits and muscle against the Welsh national side led by the midget scrum-half Dickie Owen.

77

THE ASSOCIATION Football Club at Bangor was founded in 1884 and its first encounter with Aberystwyth followed four years later. Aberystwyth versus Bangor was invariably described by correspondents as 'THE match of the season', and the fixture was governed by a mutual, obsessive desire not simply to win, but to win well. The sportsmanship ethic was invariably ignored in these fiery contests. Both sides employed reckless 'kick and rush' methods and over-zealous tackling, tripping and hacking, usually on muddy, swamp-like grounds, led to frayed tempers and bloody noses. The bulbous toe-caps on football boots, together with heavy shin guards, worn by this Bangor XI in 1895–6 (*Plate 78*), were calculated to intimidate and the game played on 22 February 1896 (which Aberystwyth won 1–0) was marred by weak refereeing and unseemly displays of bad temper. This rare photograph (*Plate 79*) displays a goalmouth scene from another encounter at Bangor on 22 February 1908. It was so wet and gusty that

78

oranges and lemons were blown off the plates before the players could consume them at the interval. Five minutes from time a 'general scrimmage' led to a winning goal for Bangor.

79

80

No one relished the hurly-burly of encounters with Bangor more than Leigh Richmond Roose (*Plate 80*), goalkeeper *par excellence*, who wore not only the colours of town and gown at Aberystwyth, but also went on to represent Druids, London Welsh, Stoke, Everton, Sunderland, Huddersfield, Aston Villa and Woolwich Arsenal. He also won twenty-four Welsh caps. An astonishingly brave, if unorthodox, goalkeeper, Roose's prodigious kicks of the ball brought gasps of admiration from admiring spectators. He could punch heavy leather balls well over the half-way line (and sometimes into distant gardens) and hesitant forwards swore that he exercised a strangely hypnotic influence over them. A dashing, irrepressible joker, 'Dick' Roose's play was quite properly described as 'of a serio-comic style'. The annual clashes with Bangor, however, often brought out the worst in him. During the tempestuous match in 1896, the following occurred: 'Before the end, an unpleasant incident happened, reflecting no credit on the feeling between the teams. Roose had run the ball out almost as far as the centre line. R.E., steering in a bee line across the field, intercepted his progress. Both went down. The Aber man, highly incensed, was up first, and at once deliberately kicked the Bangor man as the latter was in the act of rising. Gray and Fletcher naturally resented this, and Roose sought his goal in a rather knocked about condition.' By the time of his departure from College, the *Cambrian News* had exhausted its well-stocked fund of superlatives to celebrate this extraordinary player. Sadly, Roose was declared officially lost in France in October 1916.

PENURIOUS student cricketers at Bangor could not afford to buy proper equipment and were often obliged to bat and bowl on pitches more appropriate to rugby than the art perfected by Grace, Hobbes and Sutcliffe. Sartorially deficient, the 1895–6 side also fought shy of excessive physical exertion. When John Wickens took this photograph shortly before the first inter-College cricket match in May 1896, he had no need to encourage the players to adopt a languid, nonchalant pose (*Plate 81*). When they took the field, 'nervous prostration and straight bowling' did for them, and they lost by an innings and twenty runs. The student cricket correspondent unhelpfully reminded them that it was not 'absolutely bad cricket to hold a catch or two when they happen to come along'.

81

CHOPPY SEAS, biting winds or even jeering bystanders seldom dampened the zeal of boating crews, both male and female, on the Menai waters or in Cardigan Bay. Boating societies prospered in both Colleges. At Bangor a major highlight in the student calendar was the annual race between Arts and Science crews who, cheered on by the Principal, rowed in turn in a timed race from Garth jetty to the Pier buoy near Beaumaris and back again. Correspondents at Aberystwyth freely confessed that the occasional calamity was bound to occur, especially while disembarking. A female quartet, led by the intrepid Tommy Williams, came to grief in early May 1900: 'All were commanded to sit still and Tommy would row them in. They did sit still and a little too long, for as the boat grated on the beach a wave came with some force and covered half of it with its contents. A few minutes later might be seen walking along the Prom four bedraggled creatures, two holding a jacket at arm's length between them, performing the office of a watering-cart.' No doubt members of the Boating Club had learnt from bitter experience by the time this picture was taken in 1908–9 (*Plate 82*).

82

Here, with a Tennis Racquet 'neath the bough,
A Net of Balls, a Court marked out — and Thou
Before me, serving in the eventide —
And eventide were Paradise enow.

WE HAVE no means of knowing whether this parody of Kipling, penned by a lovesick student at Aberystwyth, was composed with the nubile tennis players of Bangor, pictured in 1912 in rather curious undergrowth (*Plate 83*), in mind. In spite of the wretched condition of the courts, the ladies of Bangor trounced Aberystwyth 7–2 and the Normal College 8–1 during that summer. In general, however, young women were disinclined to indulge in long, exhausting rallies, partly because their clothing inevitably restricted their mobility. Although separate clubs were formed for men and women, secretly arranged mixed doubles (played in twilight) helped to break down the barriers between the sexes.

83

MORE THAN any other College sport, ladies' hockey was bedevilled by the problem of choosing appropriate clothing. When a general meeting for hockey players was held at Aberystwyth in December 1898 in order to decide upon a suitable costume, the ensuing discussion 'drove the hapless and long-suffering chairman to the verge of distraction'. To modern eyes, the Aberystwyth ladies of 1902–3 appear ludicrously overdressed (Plate 84), but it must be borne in mind that to have appeared scantily clad on a sports field would have deeply offended the sensibilities of a puritan like Principal T. Francis Roberts (or for that matter Principal Reichel). How mobile these ladies were in the ankle-deep mud of Smithfield (known derisively as 'Smith-swamp') is hard to judge, but inter-College sporting fixtures were clearly enlivened by the clash of hockey sticks. By the time Bangor ladies posed for the camera in 1907 (Plate 85), hems had been raised an inch or two and there were some budding suffragettes in the team. Inspired by the quotation for the day in the Women Hall's Calendar ('Ye were not meant for failure but for victory') and heartened by the vociferous support of spectators, Bangor defeated Aberystwyth 2–0 on 24 February 1906.

85

84

THE BENEFITS of wholesome physical exercise were regularly preached in each of the Colleges. At Cardiff the secretary of the Gymnastic Club in 1897 urged 'hollow-eyed, weak-chested mortals, who creep about the College muttering Latin under their breath' to build up their muscles in the gymnasium. Facilities were improving and in 1908, thanks largely to the munificence and perseverance of Penry Vaughan Thomas, a fully equipped gymnasium was installed at Aberystwyth (*Plate 86*). This, in turn, led to annual exhibitions by supple students of torch swinging, rope climbing, trapeze and ring exercises. Repetitive drill exercises were now a thing of the past, for the aim, according to the Director, was to nurture 'the correct and healthy development of the body and the extension and perfection of muscular control'. The ubiquitous (see p. 53) D. J. Williams (second row, extreme left) — who was as strong as a horse — shone in these displays (*Plate 87*).

86

87

88

Few photographs of College sports meetings have survived, but an intrepid cameraman captured highlights of competitions held at Bangor cricket field on 12 May 1909, an occasion when spectators were entertained by the Royal Garrison Artillery Band as well as by lithe athletes. J. R. Davies joyfully sprinted to victory in the 120-yard race (*Plate 88*) and Ffowc Williams took the honours in the high jump by leaping 5′ 1″ (*Plate 89*). In the horizontal version, Williams travelled much further (18′ 3″) and duly won first prize. The star of the afternoon's proceedings, however, was B. F. Armitage, who received the Victor Ludorum gold medal for winning the 440 yards, 880 yards and mile.

89

90

STUDENTS were keenly competitive in sports meetings at Aberystwyth and a titanic struggle was fought in the annual Tug-of-War in May 1911 (Plate 90). Roared on by enthusiastic supporters, five teams (representing boating, gymnastics, hockey, rugby and soccer) heaved manfully against one another. In the final, the soccer team eventually succumbed to the superior strength of the boating club. Such meetings usually sported a veterans' race which, not surprisingly, attracted only a small number of entries. On warm afternoons members of staff either dozed or made their excuses and left. On 27 April 1912, however, the Welsh historian E. A. Lewis celebrated the publication of his influential *The Medieval Boroughs of Snowdonia* by storming to victory in the staff race (Plate 91). Some onlookers considered Lewis's 'run from the tennis courts to the starting point to be training within the meaning of the act', and this may account for the considerable distance between him and his nearest rivals. Among the also-rans was Teddy Eddy who, still perspiring, chaired the sports concert in the evening with characteristic good humour.

91

IN THE EARLY years, sporting events were also regularly arranged between past and present students. This hockey match was held at Bangor in 1908 (*Plate 92*). Even before the creation of the University of Wales, an Old Students' Association had been founded at Aberystwyth in March 1892. This was the brainchild of the distinguished politician Thomas Edward Ellis MP, a former Aberystwyth graduate whose commemorative statue is located in the College Quadrangle. The aim of the OSA was to enable former students to renew the fellowship of College days, to raise funds on behalf of the College, and to further the educational interests of the College and of education in Wales. Associations of past students were also founded in Bangor and Cardiff in 1898 in order to promote pride among former students in their Alma Mater and enable them to participate in a wide range of happy and money-raising social events. Each Association has flourished mightily to this day, largely as a result of the selfless labours of a small band of loyal and devoted officers and committee members.

92

OVER THE past hundred years much has been written about the debt of the Colleges to enlightened patrons, gifted academic staff, and lively and committed students. In contrast, the domestic staff are the forgotten people. This photograph of the domestic staff at Bangor (*Plate 93*), taken sometime before 1911, celebrates the hewers of wood and carriers of water – bursars, cleaners, cooks, maids, porters and many others – whose contribution to the life of the University of Wales has been supportive and ungrumbling in both good and bad times.

93

THE BUSTLE of academic and social life in the Colleges was rudely interrupted when the First World War broke out in August 1914. The mood among staff and students was optimistic, for strategists had promised a 'short war'. Members of the University Court spoke eloquently of the ideals of patriotic duty and self-sacrifice, and students responded nobly to the summons, particularly when the Military Service Act of 1915 brought about the transfer of members of the Officers' Training Corps (pictured in *Plate 94* at Aberystwyth) into the ranks of the Army. Two College Principals displayed maniacal pro-war fervour. At Cardiff Principal E. H. Griffiths expressed the view that the British Army was 'fighting savages drunk with Kultur', while Principal Reichel of Bangor declared in November 1914 that the campaign was not only for survival but also against 'scientific barbarism'. His friend and colleague, John Morris-Jones, was no less malevolent: he insisted in *Y Beirniad* that Germany had sold its soul to Lucifer.

94

LONG BEFORE 'the rush to the colours' in the war, able-bodied male students had been preparing for combat. A Volunteer Corps had been founded in Bangor as early as 1899 and, although it comprised 128 members, many of them encountered considerable difficulty in 'managing the arms and the legs properly' during intricate drills and manoeuvres. Several members of staff displayed a keen interest in military training and when the Officers' Training Corps was instituted in 1908, Principal Reichel took great pride in its activities, as indeed did Richard Williams, the tiny Assistant Registrar who, known to all and sundry as 'Dicky Sixpence', was rather unkindly described by Lewis Valentine as the man who gave 'the cold part of his heart to the English and the OTC'. Clad in khaki uniform, members of the OTC at Bangor eagerly looked forward to the annual visit to Trawsfynydd for artillery practice (*Plate 95*), though some of their student detractors were prone to inform the public that their equipment amounted to no more than one revolver, two cartridges, four small irons, six brickbats, and half a million beer bottles!

95

Merry, Merry men are we,
There's none so fair as can compare
with the boys of the O.T.C.

'PREPARE for action' was the motto of Aberystwyth students who flocked, in the first instance, to join the Volunteer detachment which, commanded by Professor Ainsworth Davies, was set up during the Boer War. In 1908 this corps was converted into a contingent of Officers' Training Corps which was licked into shape by J. W. (Jimmy) Marshall. Members attended local camps, such as that at Bow Street (*Plate 96*) or were dispatched to places like Wrexham or Ilkley or Folkestone, where squad, platoon and company drills, manoeuvres and tactical operations were interspersed with more mundane tasks like cleaning rifles, sharpening bayonets, filling bedding sacks with straw, and disposing of rations in the open air (*Plates 97–9*).

96

97

98

99

EACH COLLEGE claimed it was 'business as usual' during the war years, but academic work was undoubtedly seriously affected. The war depleted the number of male students, and women were left behind to reflect upon the appalling slaughter and the hideous physical and emotional injuries suffered by friends and loved ones. Women students at Bangor joined the Women's Service Corps in order to help with relief work, offer clerical assistance, and knit mufflers, mittens, gloves and socks, while some of their colleagues in the other two Colleges cossetted Belgian refugees, learnt first aid, and served in base and field hospitals during vacations (*Plate 100*). Such endeavours during wartime converted many of them to the cause of female suffrage. Letters received from students in the firing line or in prisoner-of-war camps sometimes conveyed images of lives brutally and tragically cut short. Such a letter was sent to D. J. Williams by Lieutenant William Thomas (a fellow gymnast!) on 21 October 1914: 'At 8.30 in the morning I had a bullet in my left shoulder and there I lay bleeding all day in a burning farm-house. No food. No help. No Williams. Nothing but hell, and that a thousand times worse than I ever dreamt it would be. At 8 p.m. the same day the Germans took me prisoner and have looked after me very well. Now I am A1, but very weak. That was a terrible day. 80 per cent of our side were killed. We were outnumbered 12 to 1 and we had no guns.'

THE CALL.

100

COMMON endeavour was not confined to the muddy trenches of Europe. Acute labour shortage and the need to increase food productivity prompted students at Bangor to roll up their sleeves and dig for victory (*Plate 101*). Additional land was brought into cultivation and allotments were extensively utilized. As the war effort made increasing demands on the time and energy of students, academic work became almost an irrelevance. As social life waned, melancholy prevailed. Inter-College sporting fixtures and debates were set aside, choral concerts (bereft of throaty bass and soaring tenor voices) were discontinued, and colourful pre-war events were allowed to pass uncelebrated. Train services were badly affected, newspapers were slimmer, and lighting restrictions deepened the sense of gloom and sadness. But at least those who stayed at home (or in College) remained sheltered from the horrors of war.

101

MEANWHILE, members of the Officers' Training Corps who awaited enlistment in the ranks continued to patrol the streets of towns and villages, (*Plate 102* reveals the Aberystwyth contingent), keep watch for spies or saboteurs, and enforce lighting restrictions. The pressure to don uniform and 'do one's bit' became intense, and most students responded courageously to the call to arms. Principal E. H. Griffiths of Cardiff was deeply moved when an English officer informed him that Welsh troops sang 'The Land of my Fathers' as they ventured 'over the top'. From the summer of 1916 onwards, however, mounting casualty lists in College handbooks testified to the slaughter, and growing numbers of students became better informed about the ghastly effects of chattering machine-gun fire, high explosive shells, viscous mud, and gas warfare. As a result, the reality of war began to be comprehended more fully. Pacifists within the student community, however, were deeply unpopular and were sometimes deplorably treated. Principal Thomas Rees of Bala-Bangor College and editor of *Y Deyrnas* bravely encouraged pacifists and conscientious objectors to express their abhorrence of war, while pacifist articles published by Welsh students in *Y Wawr* at Aberystwyth were so hostile to the war that Sir Owen M. Edwards considered them 'plain treason'.

102

MANY STUDENTS who fought with great courage and distinction found it hard, sometimes impossible, to convey the waste, horror and brutality of trench warfare. One shining exception was Robert Ronald Surtees, a Bangor student who was killed on 11 September 1916. Shortly before his death, he wrote movingly: 'The impression of the place was utterly mournful, hopeless, and devoid of life as the still things that lie between the lines – wandering bullets wail about the space like the spirit of Gawayne on the wandering wind. Yet no one can deny a glamour, and a strange eventless romanticism.' More typical was the stoical, self-deprecating humour noted on the back of the postcard (*Plate 103*) sent by former Bangor students, Major M. H. Davies, Lieutenant J. A. (Sandy) Baxter, and Lieutenant Colonel H. Lloyd Williams from Merville, France, in the summer of 1916. As they prepared for the Somme offensive, they wrote: 'As Sandy says, "Thank God, we've got a Navy!"'

103

Rolls of Honour in College magazines lengthened ominously in 1916–18 and each loss was greeted with great sadness by former mentors and colleagues. A brief reference to some of the fallen must suffice. The incomparable goalkeeper and athlete, L. R. Roose, was reported missing in October 1916 and one can only speculate whether his death resulted from another of his famous reckless dashes, this time into 'no-man's land'. Arthur Moore Lascelles of Bangor, who was killed in action in France shortly before the Armistice, was the only former student of the University of Wales to receive the Victoria Cross. David Ellis (*Plate 104*) a native of Penyfed in the parish of Llangwm and an unusually talented poet, disappeared in Macedonia in June 1918 in circumstances which have never been properly explained. His contemporaries at Bangor, including the novelist Kate Roberts, cherished fond memories of his success in gaining the College Eisteddfod Crown in 1913 for his ode 'Alltud' (*Plate 105*) and in particular of his immortal line 'Môr o jam yw Mary Jane'.

104

105

During the Great War, the British Army suffered more than 2,500,000 casualties and J. M. Staniforth drew attention to poignant losses in the student community at Cardiff (*Plate 106*). For those who lived to tell the tale, life could never be the same again. Ninety-four former students of Bangor were killed in action or died in service, and their names are commemorated in the foyer of the Prichard-Jones Hall. Aberystwyth mourned the death of 106 students and former students, while the names of 111 former students of Cardiff who perished are inscribed on a stone located outside the entrance to the Drapers' Library and unveiled by Lord Tredegar in February 1926. The acute sense of grief and desolation was best expressed in the poignant poetry of R. Williams Parry, lecturer in Welsh at Bangor. The most clumsy and gormless of soldiers, Williams Parry found solace in army camps by writing sonnets and elegies. Three graduates who died on distant battlefields were commemorated by him as follows:

From their powerless darkness, they do not see
Either sun or beauty;
Neither the tenderness of the stars,
Nor the light of the moon above their dust.

"Greater love hath no man than this: that a man lay down his life for his friends."

106

ON 12 APRIL 1916 a Royal Commission was set up to enquire into the condition of the University of Wales. The fact that the Government was prepared to carry out such a review in a period of national emergency was a measure of the urgency and importance which they attached to it. The chairman of the Commission was Richard Burdon Haldane, Viscount Haldane of Cloan. Haldane had been unjustly expelled from the Cabinet in May 1915 for alleged pro-German sympathies. But if his political commitment was undervalued, no one could question his regard for higher education and his instinctive understanding of the way in which universities worked. Haldane believed that education was 'a subject of nearly paramount importance', and on the occasion of his visit to Aberystwyth in October 1910 he had won the hearts of staff and students by speaking movingly of 'the soul of the people'. Equality of opportunity in education was an ideal which he deeply cherished and he was also known to be a firm advocate of the principle of *Lehrfreiheit*. Haldane was a cartoonist's dream. He was a portly man with an unusually large head and a penchant for making 'penguin-like gestures' whilst delivering speeches (*Plate 107*). L. S. Amery once likened him to an 'old-fashioned family butler'. Even so, this omniscient, shrewd and vastly experienced man was admirably fitted for the task in hand. He might have been the epitome of the catchphrase 'too clever by half' (Lloyd George, who was no slouch, once labelled him 'the most confusing clever man I have ever met'), but his knack of working 'caterpillar-like' at detailed administrative and organizational problems meant that the Government would have no cause to regret his appointment.

Within the University itself there was an overwhelming desire for change. Reform, perhaps even root and branch reform, was long overdue. Each of the three constituent Colleges was troubled by acute financial problems, inadequate buildings and poor facilities. Members of staff were grossly overworked and wretchedly underpaid. Even the most ardent admirers of the national University freely confessed that the Colleges were both unable and unwilling to embark on constitutional reform and that a commission was necessary. Lord Haldane headed an experienced and well-regarded team of five academics and three civil servants, two of whom (Sir Henry Jones and Sir Owen M. Edwards) were Welshmen by birth. The Commissioners (with the exception of Sir Henry Jones, Professor of Moral Philosophy at the University of Glasgow) were photographed at Cardiff in June 1916 (*Plate 108*). Standing at the rear are Sir William Osler (second from left), Regius Professor of Medicine at Oxford;

107

Professor William Henry Bragg (third from left), Quain Professor of Physics at London; Sir Owen Morgan Edwards (seventh from left), Chief Inspector of the Welsh Department of the Board of Education; Sir Alfred Daniel Hall (sixth from right), permanent adviser of the Development Commission; William Napier Bruce (second from right), son of Lord Aberdare and Principal Assistant Secretary to the Board of Education; Dr William Henry Hadow, Principal of Armstrong College, Durham. Seated are Lord Haldane (centre) and to his left Miss Emily Penrose, Principal of Somerville College, Oxford. Sir Isambard Owen ventured the opinion that the team constituted 'the ablest University Commission . . . that I have known in my time'. Its brief was 'to inquire into the organisation and work of the University of Wales and its three constituent Colleges, and into the

108

relations of the University to those Colleges and to other institutions in Wales providing education of a post-secondary nature, and to consider in what respects the present organisation of University Education in Wales can be improved and what changes, if any, are desirable in the constitution, function, and powers of the University and its three Colleges'. Haldane likened his mission to 'a voyage of discovery' and he and his colleagues threw themselves enthusiastically into the task. Over a period of nearly two years the Commission held thirty-one sittings, during which oral evidence was delivered by 156 witnesses, and thirty-six sittings for its own members. Its final report, published in March 1918, is packed with information for historians who relish telling detail. Although it was much less radical than many had predicted, it contained a number of original and inventive recommendations which helped to strengthen both the public image and the Welshness of the University. The principle of a single national university was firmly endorsed, but a considerable measure of independence in teaching matters was delegated to the individual Colleges. Comprehensive, judicious and far-seeing, the report carried great conviction and was widely praised. Since most of the Commissioners' recommendations were incorporated in the Supplemental Charter of 1920, there can be no doubt that the Haldane Report marked a new epoch in the history of the University of Wales.

THE FIRST casualty of the remodelling process was the University Senate, pictured in *Plate 109* in its valedictory sitting on 29 September 1920. By the time of the Royal Commission, the Senate had few admirers. Some dubbed it a dinosaur, while others claimed it was a law unto itself. It was large, cumbersome and unwieldy, so much so that one newspaper offered the view that it was in serious danger of strangling itself in its own red tape. Principal E. H. Griffiths facetiously commented that guiding the Ten Commandments through the Senate would take at least nineteen months! Sir Owen M. Edwards was convinced that most of its members nursed an anti-Welsh animus and could not be relied upon to champion the principle of federalism. The Royal Commission therefore recommended that it be disbanded and replaced by a seventeen-strong Academic Board charged with the responsibility of providing another new body, the University Council, with expert information and advice on academic matters. The four Principals (A. H. Trow of Cardiff, H. R. Reichel of Bangor, J. H. Davies of Aberystwyth and T. F. Sibly of Swansea), seated next to the Secretary, Miss M. E. Pearson, look suitably glum, and judging by the expression of their colleagues few members of Senate were happy to call the new world into existence.

109

HALDANE and his fellow Commissioners were also acutely conscious of the need to invigorate the University Court, to make it more democratic, and to render it 'a mirror of the national mind'. Haldane himself was much taken by a spirited proposal by Gwyneddon Davies, representing the Caernarfonshire Education Authority, that the Court should travel, Bedouin-like, to different parts of Wales and set itself up as a national festival or, in Haldane's words, 'a Parliament of Higher Education'. It was recommended that its membership should increase from 108 to 213 and that it should meet, *pace* the National Eisteddfod, at least once a year for the best part of six days to discuss University business and formulate plans for the development of higher education. Mercifully, perhaps, Haldane's wildly extravagant hopes for the Court were never fully realized, but it did become more representative and more accountable to the public. The first meeting of the reconstituted Court was held at Swansea on 23 November 1921. In *Plate 110* Principals Reichel (Bangor), Trow (Cardiff) and Sibly (Swansea) escort the new Pro-Chancellor, Lord Kenyon, while *Plate 111* reveals a posse of lady students greeting the University dignitaries with a rousing cheer.

111

110

HALDANE'S Commission gave a fresh impetus to the fortunes of adult education by recommending that a University Extension Board be set up to review, co-ordinate and assist extra-mural work in the four Welsh Colleges. Initiatives in this field had been curtailed by the war but, as Haldane had anticipated, the coming of peace stimulated new demands for evening classes from a wide range of social groups. Large numbers of men and women were anxious to make intelligent use of leisure time, sharpen their intellects, and forward their careers. By 1923–4, 2,555 students had enrolled in sixty-four tutorial classes and thirty-two pioneer classes. From the outset, the emphasis was placed on Socratic dialogue, mutual respect between tutor and students, frank exchange of views, and the maximum amount of purposeful enjoyment. From the 1920s onwards, government initiatives, demographic changes, and increased public demand for a liberal education all helped to encourage the growth of adult education. Summer schools and rallies prospered as never before (*Plate 112*). By 1989–90 a record number of 24,159 students were attending 1,332 classes at the four Welsh Colleges of Aberystwyth, Bangor, Cardiff and Swansea, and there is no doubt that the University of Wales can be proud of its achievement in widening the horizons and enriching the lives of mature students.

112

MEMBERS OF Haldane's Royal Commission were acutely concerned about what they referred to as 'the want of zeal and initiative' in promoting Celtic Studies. Evidence presented to them by Principal J. H. Davies and Principal Reichel had convinced them that the University should bestir itself and it was therefore recommended that a University Board of Celtic Studies, consisting of fifteen members, be set up to organize postgraduate studies, co-ordinate research, and publish its results. Under the Supplemental Charter of 1920 a Board was duly established, and three committees – Welsh Language and Literature, History and Law, and Archaeology and Art – were set up to devise a programme of research and publication. A Social Sciences Committee was added to this triumvirate in 1969. The first number of the academic journal, *The Bulletin of the Board of Celtic Studies*, edited by Professor J. E. Lloyd, Professor Ifor Williams, and Dr Mortimer Wheeler, was published in 1922 at five shillings to subscribers. The journal still prospers. The Board has also published valuable textual and critical editions of Welsh poetry and prose, studies of archaeology, history, politics and sociology. Two of its most outstanding recent projects are *Geiriadur Prifysgol Cymru* (*The University of Wales Dictionary*), which is expected to be completed by the end of the twentieth century, and *The National Atlas of Wales*, edited by Professor Harold Carter and published in four instalments by the University of Wales Press between 1981 and 1989. *Plate 113* shows Professor Harold Carter and Mr Harry Griffiths with the John Bartholomew Award of the British Cartographic Society, an award which acknowledges excellence in the field of small-scale thematic cartography. In many ways, the Board affords a notably successful example of the benefits of inter-collegiate activity within the University.

113

AMONG THE most novel and intriguing recommendations of the Royal Commission was that a University Press be established. In the event, no printing press as such was set up, but the University Press Board, which was first convened in London in January 1922, began to operate as the publishing house of the University. Over the past seventy years, the Press has published a wide range of titles, notably in the field of Celtic scholarship, and has at present a backlist of over five hundred titles (*Plate 114*). Several of its most valuable issues have been published on behalf of the University Board of Celtic Studies. Initially housed in the University Registry in Cathays Park, in 1975 the Press was found a permanent headquarters in Gwennyth Street where energetic preparations are at present under way for new and exciting expansion in publishing activities.

114

ONE OF THE most imaginative recommendations of the Royal Commission was associated with the musical culture of Wales. At the instigation of Sir Henry Hadow (who believed that Wales as a musical nation was 'an unworked gold-mine'), the Commission recommended that departments of music be established in each College and that a Council of Music, led by a Director, should harness the musical resources of Wales. In 1918 Henry Walford Davies (*Plate 115*) a native of Oswestry and an extremely gifted organist and conductor, was elected to the Chair of Music at Aberystwyth and Director of the National Council of Music for the University of Wales. Walford Davies was a born communicator, and the twin appointments marked a new era in the musical life of Wales. No one did more in the inter-war period to educate the musically illiterate and to encourage the humblest to sing and play. He was fond of quoting Gustav Holst's observation that music was the 'natural and universal language' of all but two in every thousand human beings. By setting up music clubs, lecture concerts, summer schools and festivals, by founding orchestras and choral unions, and by inviting celebrated conductors like Adrian Boult, Gustav Holst and Sir Henry Wood to mid

115

Wales, Davies brought music to the attention of people who seldom attended concerts or listened to music (*Plate 116*). Walford Davies had a real love for music and a great affection for musicians, both amateur and professional. A natural raconteur, he delighted in telling long and often complicated stories about his musical acquaintances and of his efforts to assist Gwendoline and Margaret Davies, philanthropists *par excellence*, in making Gregynog the most celebrated music-making centre in mid Wales. His exhibitionism and razzmatazz were not to the taste of all musical purists and there were some complaints that he was more than adept in getting his own way. But his students were totally devoted to him. His organizational talent, prodigious energy and infectious enthusiasm enabled him to establish and maintain a rapport with them, and they often responded following concerts by carrying him shoulder high around the Quad. News of his knighthood in 1922 was joyfully received in Aberystwyth, but four years later ill health forced him to retire from the Chair, though he continued his duties as Director of Music for the University of Wales.

116

EVER SINCE the foundation of Departments of Anatomy and Physiology in Cardiff College in 1893, the establishment of a fully-fledged medical school had been a topic of lively conversation in academic circles. But when Haldane's Commission grasped the nettle by recommending the setting up of a National Medical School for Wales as an independent constituent college of the University, thereby severing its links with the College at Cardiff, there was furious controversy. The anti-separation lobby spoke loudly of 'betrayal', 'dismemberment' and 'leading Wales downhill'. For their part, pro-separationists argued that the progeny had outgrown its nest. It could no longer operate effectively under the cumbrous administrative aegis of the University College and it required greater scope to develop. When details of a charter and statutes were finally resolved, three new professors were appointed in readiness for the opening of the

117

118

Medical School in October 1921, among them A. M. (Jock) Kennedy (*Plate 117*), first Professor of Medicine in the University of Wales and Director of the Professorial Medical Unit at the Cardiff Royal Infirmary. But acute differences of opinion continued to fester, and the so-called 'School of Medicine Affair' was a recurring feature in the columns of the south Wales press until 1931. Every attempt by leading Welsh educationists to seek a settlement was thwarted, and the whole controversy was beset with what newspaper reporters dubbed 'awkward dilemmas', 'fears of disaster' and 'fateful decisions'. The matter became thoroughly unpleasant when, in 1927, the authorities at Cardiff College prepared to take steps to protect the legal rights of their institution. Suing the University was unheard of, and, mercifully, such an event failed to materialize. Relations between the two institutions, however, remained strained and unhappy until 1931 when the School of Medicine was finally granted by Supplemental Charter control of all clinical subjects within an autonomous School of the University. The first Provost of the School was Colonel Alfred William Sheen (1869–1945) (*Plate 118*), a native of Cardiff and the first Professor of Surgery at the School of Medicine. From 1 July 1931, therefore, the Welsh National School of Medicine began life as a separate institution.

ONE OF THE most welcome recommendations of the Royal Commission was that the College at Swansea be admitted into the University of Wales. Ever since the Aberdare Report of 1881, Swansea had entertained fond hopes of establishing a fully-fledged university college. The rebuff suffered in 1883, when Cardiff became the South Wales College, was both painful and humiliating to the promoters of Swansea's cause. Licking their wounds, they retired to their tents to await better days. In the mean time, technical classes were established and by 1901 a Technical College, maintained by the local authority, had been founded. When champions of the university cause scented a change in the wind with the setting up of the Royal Commission in 1916, a powerful case was presented to the Commissioners, based largely on the reputation of Swansea as the metallurgical metropolis of the kingdom. Members of the Commission made it clear, however, that Swansea's elevation to the rank of university would be dependent on its ability to establish an endowment fund of up to £40,000 in order to pay adequate salaries to professors and establish a faculty of arts. To their credit, local industrialists and businessmen rallied to the support of the College and by the end of November 1917 the princely sum of £71,000 had been raised. When the Haldane Commission enthusiastically endorsed Swansea's application, the Privy Council lost no time in giving its blessing to the incorporation of the new college into the University of Wales. On 19 July 1920 – a gloriously sunny day – King George V, Queen Mary and Princess Mary visited Swansea. At Singleton Park a royal dais, with a brilliant scarlet canopy, had been set under the trees in the parkland (*Plate 119*). Here the King was presented with a splendid welcome scroll (*Plate 120*). It was here, too, that the King laid the foundation stone of the new buildings and presented to Frank W. Gilbertson, President of the College, the first Charter of the College. In his address, the King expressed the following sentiments: 'It will be the task of your College to send out into the world men and women fully equipped for the material work which awaits them, and with minds attuned to high ideals, opened to the rich and varied interests of modern life, and steadfastly set towards the service of their followers.'

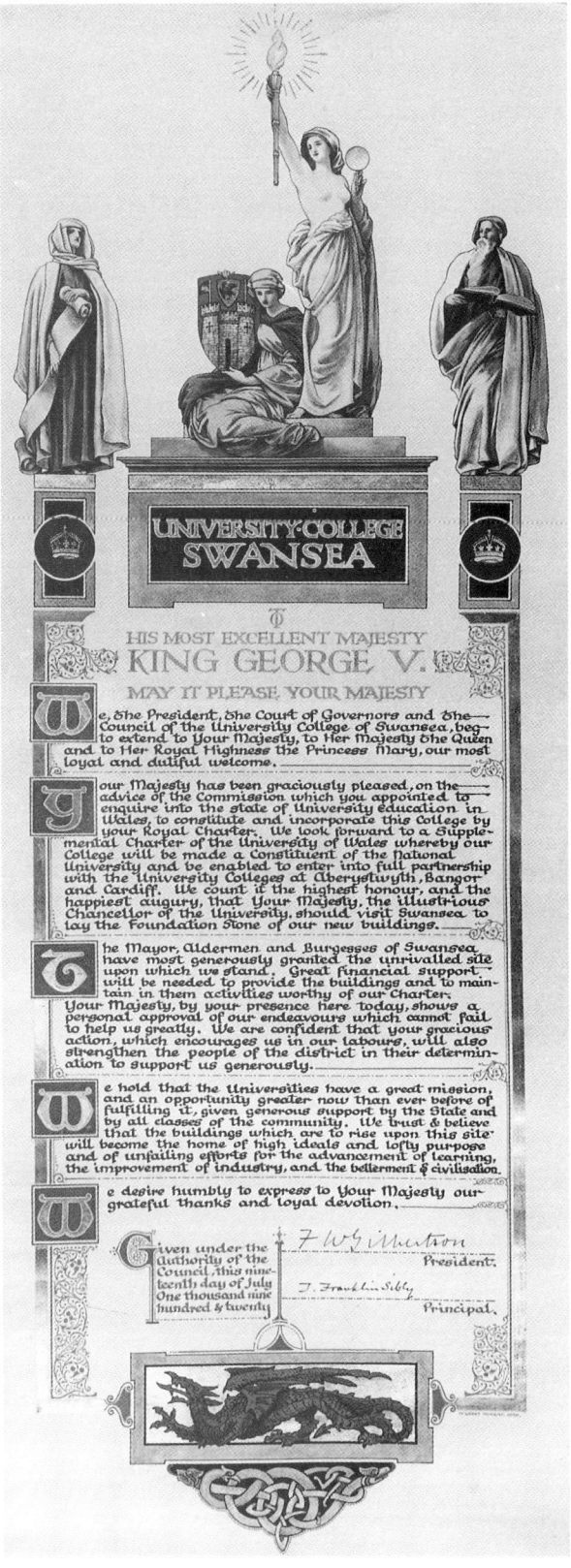

120

119

AMONG THE dignitaries introduced to King George V on 19 July was Richard Martin, 'the father of the university movement in Swansea' (Plate 121). Following a brief education at the Hafod Copper Works' school, Martin had spent some time as a clerk in Grimsby before setting up the Vale of Swansea zinc works at Llansamlet. A town councillor in Swansea since 1884, Martin became the most influential and popular promoter of the special claims of the Technical College for admittance to the University of Wales. As he approached the dais in Singleton Park, loud cries of 'Good old Dick Martin' rang out. He was later knighted for his public services.

121

SINGLETON Abbey, which now houses the administrative offices of the University College of Swansea, became the first home of the fledgeling college (*Plate 122*). The original owners of this neo-Gothic pile were the prodigiously wealthy Vivian family, Swansea's most celebrated industrial dynasty. In February 1896 virtually the whole of the north wing had been destroyed by a raging fire, and when the building was eventually placed on the market in the spring of 1919 it was in a state of serious disrepair. But the potential was evident for those with eyes to see, and the site was swiftly snapped up by the Corporation. Negotiations then began between town and gown. Unfortunately, acrimony and bitterness ensued, and nothing had been permanently resolved by the time the royal party visited the site in July 1920. Presumably King George V was informed that the foundation stone which he had laid to rest might eventually find a permanent home elsewhere. College leaders were furious at what they believed was the treacherous reluctance of the Corporation to be true to its word. All was not lost, however, for in December 1920 the Corporation presented Singleton to the College at a nominal rent until a more permanent site was secured in the park. In August 1923 Singleton Abbey and nineteen acres of adjoining land were finally donated as a permanent site to the College, together with fifteen acres to the west of Sketty Lane for use as playing fields.

122

THE EARLY years were a struggle for survival at Swansea. Financial problems, ramshackle buildings, makeshift facilities, a skeleton staff and a tiny student body made it hard for both staff and students to hold their heads high. It was as well that the first Principal, Dr Thomas Franklin Sibly, refused to let morale waver (*Plate 123*). Sibly's candidature had been endorsed by Lord Haldane, who had been impressed both by Sibly's graciousness and the force of his arguments at the time of the Royal Commission sittings. The former Professor of Geology at Cardiff (1913–18) and Armstrong College, Newcastle-upon-Tyne (1918–20), Sibly beat off the challenge of five other applicants and accepted the post of Principal with an annual salary of £1500. Still only thirty-five, he showed from the outset great tact, good sense and firmness in his dealings with Swansea Corporation and in forging close links with local industrialists. An able administrator and a fine speaker, he worked tirelessly in order to raise the profile of the College and by the time of his resignation in 1926 its fortunes had improved enormously.

123

ONE OF Principal Sibly's dreams was to establish at Swansea the finest metallurgical school in Europe. He was determined to launch initiatives that would ensure that the College would be of service to the industrial community and that local manufacturers, coalowners and industrialists would recognize that metallurgy was the 'characteristic speciality' of the College. By 1923 fully equipped laboratories and workshops had been provided for metallurgy, physics and chemistry. The metallurgy laboratory was reckoned to be the best equipped in Wales (Plate 124), and it is significant that Dr C. A. Edwards, Professor of Metallurgy and Vice-Principal, commanded a salary of £1250 per annum, a substantially larger stipend than other professors in the College.

124

WHEN THE first academic session began in Swansea on 5 October 1920, there were five science departments but only one lecturer – Ernest Hughes, Head of History – representing the arts. Hughes could justifiably claim: 'I am the Faculty of Arts!' By the second session, however, new appointments had been made in the faculty. One of the most notable was Dr Mary Rhiannon Williams, Reader in Romance Philology in the University of London who, in 1921, was made Head of the Department of Modern Languages and Professor of French Language and Literature. Professor Williams was the first woman appointed to a university chair in Britain. By a strange quirk of fortune, Dr G. Arbour Stevens, who had violently opposed her appointment (on shamelessly sexist grounds), married her four years later! In 1934 the President of France conferred upon Mary Williams the distinction of Chevalier de la Légion d'Honneur. Mary Williams is pictured here (*Plate 125*) in old age. She died, aged ninety-four, in 1977.

125

When Principal Sibly left to become Principal of the University of London at the end of the 1925–6 session, the College was in a much stronger position. With pardonable exaggeration, his deputy and successor, Principal C. A. Edwards, referred to the 'phenomenal progress' made by the College since 1920. By 1926 every department in the College had been allocated a permanent home in Singleton Park, though some of the stuffier members of staff resented having to share the parkland with grazing cattle and horses! The complement of staff increased from eighteen in 1920–1 to forty-four in 1926–7 and sixty-five in 1938–9. Among the luminaries in *Plate 126*, a photograph taken in 1926, are J. Saunders Lewis (back row, extreme left), Professor C. A. Edwards and Principal Sibly (middle row, respectively eleventh and twelfth from left), Professor D. Emrys Evans (Head of Classics and later Principal of Bangor, front row, fifth from right), Professor Henry Lewis (Head of Welsh, front row, second from right) and Professor F. A. Cavenagh (Head of Education, front row, extreme right).

126

THE ECONOMIST E. F. Schumacher has assured us that 'small is beautiful', and there was certainly a strong *esprit de corps* in Wales's youngest constituent College at Swansea. Only eighty-nine full-time students (of whom eight were women) enrolled in the first session of 1920–1. Fifty-five of these had been students at the Technical College. Both association football and rugby teams were dogged by manpower problems and only with great difficulty were teams raised in order to honour fixtures. Recreational and social facilities were lamentable. From time to time staff and students filled their leisure hours by attending social gatherings on the archery lawn, and dancing classes conducted on Saturday evenings were not unpopular. By 1921 a companion to *Omnibus*, *The Dragon*, and *Cap and Gown*, had arrived on the scene. *The Undergraduate* (*Plate 127*), launched and maintained by a small group of enthusiasts, not only helped to bind the tiny student community together but also displayed a commendable readiness to collaborate with its sister magazines in other Colleges. By 1925–6 the student cohort had increased to 382 (including 145 women), of whom 64 per cent lived at home and travelled daily to College to pursue their studies. *Plate 128* reveals former pupils of Ystalyfera county school, pictured c.1921 outside Singleton Abbey in the company of Professor Henry Lewis and Professor Emrys Evans.

127

128

IN SPITE of the remodelling of the University in response to the recommendations of the Royal Commission, there were still many vociferous critics of the University. The charge that it had failed the nation never staled with repetition. At a bardic ceremony in Caernarfon in June 1920, Llew Tegid (*Plate 129*) publicly indicted the University for sacrificing Welshness on the altar of English values. The report of his speech in the *Western Mail* ran as follows: 'The Eisteddfod had reared eminent Welsh talent – had the Welsh University done so? Had the colleges since they became associated in an university produced even one really great man? (*Applause*). It was true that Aberystwyth College had done so, but that was before it became a component part of the university. During the twelve years of its independent existence it had raised really great men. (*Applause*). But while the colleges had been at work for nearly forty years what could they show as the fruit of their work in producing great men?' On his return from the battlefields of Europe, Lewis Valentine roundly condemned the Colleges for conducting their academic and administrative affairs in English, while the Reverend Thomas Rees, Principal of Coleg Bala-Bangor, voiced the need for Celtic scholarship to be taught not 'as a dead language' but 'on the basis of the spoken language'. In 1925 Alderman William George of Cricieth (brother of Lloyd George) scathingly announced that the University of Wales was a non-Welsh institution since it made little or no effort to provide leadership in those cultural matters which the nation cherished.

129

130

FOLLOWING the reconstitution of the University in 1920, a number of changes in personnel occurred. When King George V retired as Chancellor and accepted the title of Protector, Edward Albert, Prince of Wales (later King Edward VIII) was elected Chancellor on 4 February 1921, a post which he held until 1936. A message of welcome (presumably unsent) from Bangor students read as follows: 'To HRH the Prince of Wales: Dear Old Chap, Congrats old bean on having come a member of the finest old University in the world.' On 8 June the Prince was officially installed as Chancellor during a dignified ceremony in the Empire Theatre, Cardiff. *Plate 130* reveals him in his robes, together with his train-bearer, Lord John Crichton-Stuart, son of the Marquis and Marchioness of Bute. The new Chancellor was kept busy. On a grey, rainy day in late October 1923, he arrived in Aberystwyth to declare open the new Students' Union in the handsome Old Assembly Rooms in Laura Place. Students attached ropes to the front of his Rolls Royce and, to deafening cheers, pulled the car through the streets. In *Plate 131* he is escorted by Principal J. H. Davies and Lord Davies, Senior Vice-President of the College, to the Union. Following his speech, four muscular student

131

athletes hoisted the Prince shoulder high and carried him to his car. The following day, 1 November, the Prince travelled to Bangor to open the Memorial Arch which commemorated the 8,500 soldiers, sailors and airmen of north Wales who fell during the Great War. Located at the south-west corner of the College Park, the Arch had been erected at a total cost of £15,000. It proved a poignant occasion for the 10,000 people who assembled in the Park, and tears flowed freely when the specially commissioned hymn by R. Williams Parry, set to music by E. T. Davies, was sung:

> Arglwydd, O gwêl ein meirw drud,
>   A derbyn hwy i gôl dy dadol hedd;
> I orffwys aethant ennyd fer o'r byd
>   I'r bedd.

The Prince subsequently laid the foundation stone of the new Science Memorial Buildings which were duly opened, three years later, by the celebrated physicist Sir J. J. Thomson. In spite of a heavy police presence (students complained that recruiting 'the fattest bobbies' in north Wales did not ease the congestion), the Prince was subjected to more boisterous ragging. A mock court ceremony was organized in which he was installed as a freeman of the University, which enabled him to use the College tower free of rent, attend Senate tax-free, have access to the chemistry laboratories, smoke freely in the main corridor, be exempt from College dinners, and apply for any degree of his choice. The 'lady mayoress' (Bowen Thomas, President of the Students' Representative Council) then presented him with a golden casket containing a silver-mounted hunting crop and cigarettes (*Plate 132*).

132

IN NOVEMBER 1927 the University lost one of its doughtiest champions when Lloyd Tyrrell Kenyon, Baron Kenyon (Plate 133), died of pleurisy and typhoid (caused by a mosquito bite). Known as 'the tallest peer of his generation', Lord Kenyon could easily have been mistaken for a bucolic country gentleman. In fact, he was an uncommonly able administrator who rendered valuable service to the University as Senior-Deputy Chancellor 1910–20 and Pro-Chancellor 1920–7. To his office Kenyon brought selfless commitment, administrative exactness and considerable shrewdness. His lugubrious features masked an engaging bonhomie and a capacity to inspire others to devote themselves to the welfare of the University.

133

134

THE INTER-WAR years witnessed jubilee celebrations in each of the three original constituent Colleges. First in line was Aberystwyth in 1922. At Easter hundreds of former students returned to the town to partake in the festivities, to re-live 'the Aber Spirit', and to raise funds in aid of a memorial for fallen heroes. More highlights followed in July. On the nineteenth the whole town, according to the *Western Mail*, was 'palpitating with agreeable excitement'. The hubbub was caused by the impending arrival of David Lloyd George who, as always, was accorded a tumultuous reception. As an aperitif, the College had organized the unveiling of a bronze statue of Principal Thomas

135

Charles Edwards. Designed by Sir William Goscombe John, the statue was not a particularly faithful likeness of the first Principal (onlookers queried the wisdom of dispensing with the Principal's spectacles!). At any rate, the unveiling ceremony went without a hitch and was performed with great dignity by Mrs Edward Davies, Plas Dinam (*Plate 134*). On the same day, Lloyd George was made an honorary freeman of the borough of Aberystwyth. In his speech, delivered before 2,500 delirious supporters in the College Hall, he told the tale of an old woman who (long after Principal Thomas Charles Edwards had retired) still kept a half crown in a glass in readiness for his personal fund-raising visit. A former student recalled the occasion vividly: 'I can see the old rogue now, as he stood there before us on the broad, sunlit platform – his shining white hair, his pink cheeks, his beautifully-cut grey suit, his small, gleaming shoes. From top to toe he was all smiling, twinkling charm as he spoke, now with a light jest, now in a tone of sober gravity, but always with perfect assurance and effortless mastery' (*Plate 135*). On 9 October the celebrations were rounded off with a joint meeting of the Court of Governors, Council, Senate, Students' Representative Council and Old Students' Association Committees, during which Mr Evan Evans, clerk of the County Council, and the only person present who had witnessed the opening of the College in 1872, acknowledged the nation's debt to the founding fathers. Tea was served afterwards to over 300 guests in the Quad and Examination Hall (*Plate 136*).

136

THE WELSH Colleges were not immune from the debilitating effects of the slump following the First World War and, as this cartoon in the *South Wales Daily News* vividly suggests (*Plate 137*), the financial position at Cardiff was extremely gloomy. Substantial bank overdrafts were a heavy burden and in 1921 a public appeal for £250,000 was launched. The most generous donation came from the shipowner William James Tatem, Lord Glanely, President of the College 1919–24. Lord Glanely contributed the handsome sum of £85,000 for the Tatem Chemistry and Physics Laboratories and for agricultural buildings. But the general response from industrialists in Glamorgan was disappointing, and by 1938 income from endowments in the College was less than £3,000.

137

During the 'locust years' of the 1930s, Cardiff had good cause to be grateful to Sir Montague Burton, the affluent Lithuanian Jew who was the head of the biggest and most successful manufacturing and retail clothing business in the world. Burton was both deeply interested in intellectual matters and in the welfare of labouring people, and in 1930 he donated £20,000 to endow a Chair of Industrial Relations at Cardiff. Its first occupant was a native of Cardiff and a graduate of Cardiff. Aged twenty-nine, Hilary A. Marquand became the youngest University Professor in Wales (*Plate 138*). He immediately laid plans to set Wales on the road to industrial recovery. In his celebrated survey, 'South Wales Needs a Plan', he perceived the need for united action in identifying the major economic requirements of the area, in attracting new industries, and in stimulating co-operative action.

Even at a time of large-scale unemployment, when thousands of Welsh people either stood idly on street corners or left their homeland in search of regular work, Hilary Marquand was never less than optimistic, as this postcard (*Plate 139*) sent by him

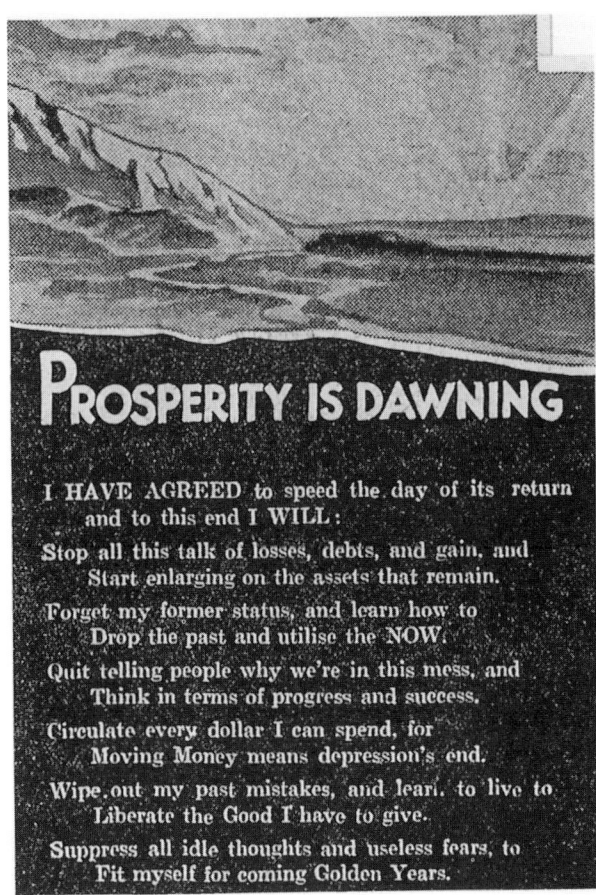

139

138

from Los Angeles to Principal J. F. Rees, indicates. He encouraged students to organize holiday summer camps for unemployed men, where sports and recreations, bathing parades and camp-fire concerts not only brought colour and variety to the drab lives of the unemployed but also provided students with valuable training and experience. Many students, however, were themselves in serious financial difficulties and were scarcely able to maintain themselves because their fathers were ill or unemployed. Loan funds established in Colleges were lamentably inadequate and it is significant that the proportion of women students entering the University of Wales declined sharply during the 1930s.

AT A TIME when unemployment figures were rising alarmingly, the University was not slow to acknowledge the efforts of those on the dole to seek solace and profit in the world of books. It won universal acclaim in 1931 by awarding an honorary MA to Bob Owen, Croesor (1885–1962) (*Plate 140*), an unemployed quarryman. This extraordinary bibliophile, genealogist, historian, lecturer and broadcaster was a legendary figure. He cultivated an obsessive taste for rare books and his collection (possibly numbering 50,000) was packed into every nook and cranny of his home in Croesor. This tiny, restless, noisy man possessed, in the words of Philip O'Connor, 'a child's candour, a warlock's shrewdness, and a poet's entrancement with all living things'. Owen treasured the memory of the degree ceremony at Swansea: 'I remember the capping day as if it were yesterday. The applause never stopped from the moment Professor Ernest Hughes came to escort me from my seat until I had reached the platform. I got a better reception than anyone – for the simple reason, of course, that I was unemployed.'

140

ALTHOUGH there was little in the financial affairs of Cardiff to inspire confidence and rejoice the heart, there were happy celebrations on the occasion of its half centenary in the summer of 1933. On 19 July the Bute family played host to a well-attended garden party in the Castle Grounds, and on the following day around 2,500 guests attended the Congregation of the University at Greyfriars Hall. To celebrate the Jubilee, a valuable summary of factual and statistical information was compiled by A. H. Trow and D. J. A. Brown, entitled *A Short History of the College, 1883 to 1933*. Among those present at the celebrations were student number 1 on the roll, Charles Edward Williams of Cardiff, and student number 10,000, John Norman Thomas (*Plate 141*). Among the most memorable accounts of the blessings which Cardiff conferred upon its alumni is that by Professor Gwyn Jones, who entered the College in 1924: 'My years in College seemed to me then, and impress me still, as pure magic. They widened my horizons, extended my acquaintance, honed my perceptions, and supplied me with models to emulate or decline. By examples noble, endearing, and sometimes mildly daft, they helped my mind cohere.'

141

During 1922, the year of its Jubilee celebrations, the College at Aberystwyth had erected a University College Hall. A reconstructed aircraft hangar, it was the only building in the town capable of accommodating up to 3,000 people and it became the venue not only for lively concerts organized by Walford Davies but also memorable speeches by Lloyd George, Stanley Baldwin and George Lansbury. On a hot Sunday evening in August 1933, however, a raging fire razed the combustible wooden building to the ground in little more than thirty minutes (*Plate 142*). Firefighters, poorly served by inadequate appliances and hydrants, were unable to check the progress of the fire. It was another catastrophic event in the history of the College, and staff and students alike could easily have been forgiven for wondering whether successive scourges were the will of the Almighty.

142

143

144

A VERY DIFFERENT and more celebrated fire inflamed passions three years later. On 8 September 1936, Saunders Lewis, poet, playwright, literary critic, lecturer in Welsh at Swansea, and President of Plaid Genedlaethol Cymru, D. J. Williams, schoolteacher, short-story writer, and a graduate of the University, and Lewis Valentine, Baptist minister and also a graduate of the University, deliberately set fire to a RAF bombing school at Penyberth in Llŷn before giving themselves up to the police (Plate 143). At Caernarfon Assizes the jury failed to agree on a verdict and, much to the disapproval of large sections of Welsh society, the case was transferred to the Old Bailey where the three patriots were sentenced to nine months' imprisonment. In his address to the jury at Caernarfon, Saunders Lewis claimed that his action at Penyberth had protected 'the honour of the University of Wales, for the language and literature of Wales are the very *raison d'être* of this University'.

The 'Fire in Llŷn' and its consequences were furiously and passionately debated, and the issue placed not only the College at Swansea but also the University under the microscope. To fervent nationalists, the three arsonists were patriots and heroes, but in the eyes of the majority of members of the College Council at Swansea the conduct of Saunders Lewis had been wilfully irresponsible and his appointment was terminated on 19 January 1937. This peremptory action immediately incurred the wrath of many academics, though it is worth noting that Professor Henry Lewis, Head of the Department of Welsh, made no attempt to conceal his contempt for Lewis's behaviour and duly voted for his removal from his post as lecturer. An avalanche of petitions in favour of reinstating Lewis was ignored, and during an angry protest meeting in Swansea on 22 May 1937 (*Plate 144*), the chairman, Walter Jones, described the College Council as 'a mixture of ignoramuses and traitors, a contemptible lot of ruffians'. In spite of an impassioned plea by Griffith John Williams, representing the Guild of Graduates, and a petition signed by 300 students, the Court of the University of Wales in July 1937 resolved on constitutional grounds to take no action. The widespread sense of sorrow and anger was best expressed by R. Williams Parry in his poem 'Y Gwrthodedig' (The Rejected);

Dear country, if you can dispense with the learning
Of the most learned one amongst us,
You must be, of all countries,
The most fortunately endowed.

In 1952, however, the prodigal son re-entered the University fold when he was appointed to teach Welsh at Cardiff. The honorary D.Litt. conferred upon Saunders Lewis by the University of Wales in 1983 was an act of atonement as well as an acknowledgement of his genius.

DISTINGUISHED members of staff in the interwar years continued to adorn University life. If there was acute concern regarding the Welshness of the University, there was nothing but admiration and praise for its principal authorities on Welsh language and literature. From 1895 to 1929 the Chair of Welsh at Bangor was occupied by Sir John Morris-Jones (he was knighted in 1918). Poet, critic and scholar, Morris-Jones was a pioneer in Welsh orthography and prosody. His *A Welsh Grammar, Historical and Comparative* (1913) established his reputation as a supremely gifted philologist, while *Cerdd Dafod* (1925) confirmed that here indeed was a master of the intricacies of the traditional Welsh metres. According to W. J. Gruffydd, the work he accomplished 'was nothing less than the restoration of a civilization which had been lost and forgotten'. More than any other Welsh scholar of his day, he had rehabilitated the Welsh language and shown it to be a European language worthy of honour and esteem. In spite of his vast learning, Sir John Morris-Jones never lost the common touch: working people came in their hundreds to his public lectures and his adjudications at National Eisteddfodau were spellbinding. *Plate 145* reveals him (extreme right) in the company of Henry Lewis, Professor of Welsh at Swansea (left), and the Reverend Fred Jones (foreground).

145

THE DEPARTMENT of Welsh at Aberystwyth, too, was blessed with a man of multiple gifts and interests. Sir Thomas H. Parry-Williams (he was knighted in 1958) was one of the most creative and versatile figures in the history of the University of Wales. Educated at Aberystwyth, he graduated in Welsh in 1908 and in Latin in 1909. He then pursued philological studies at Oxford, Freiburg and Paris. In 1912 he stunned the nation by winning the coveted Crown and Chair at the Wrexham National Eisteddfod and, to even greater popular acclaim, nonchalantly repeated the feat at Bangor three years later. In 1914 he was appointed lecturer in Welsh at Aberystwyth, but when his name was recommended to the College Council in 1920 as a fit person to fill the Chair of Welsh a storm of protest arose among those who had resented Parry-Williams's stand against militarism during the Great War. Deeply wounded by this rebuff, he enrolled as a medical student and astonished his peers by winning the coveted Tom Jones Award in Surgery. He was

146

then invited to fill the Chair of Welsh which he held until his retirement in 1952. During these creative years he enthralled the nation with an array of elegant essays and sonorous poems, many of which focused on his longing for his beloved Snowdonia and on the meaning of life and death. He was, in many ways, the first truly modern Welsh poet. This genuinely modest and intensely private man was never less than inspirational in class, and his unique teaching style has been brilliantly described by Brinley Rees: 'His students, when they recall the trim gowned figure standing at his reading-desk on its corner platform or flitting with light step to make seductive use of the blackboard, will remember not only the shy, boyish smile and the look of mischief in his eye but also the obvious delight in the fit and feel of speech-sounds, the care in seeking to convey the nuance of word or phrase, the timbre and integrity of his reading and the unmistakable sensitivity which, not being touchiness, implied a due regard for the singularity of other persons.' In *Plate 146* he proudly displays his companion KC 16, a two-year old motor bike which he bought in September 1920, while *Plate 147* reveals the public figure in old age.

147

148

D URING the inter-war period there were fewer eccentrics on the staff to entertain and baffle impressionable students. Even so, some well-regarded academics nursed decidedly odd traits. H. J. Fleure, the Guernsey-born Professor of Geography and Anthropology at Aberystwyth (1918–33) liked to welcome members of the public to his classes and organize field trips, excursions and picnics partly because his main preoccupation was the story of physical and cultural evolution. *Plate 148* reveals him, standing left, together with E. G. Bowen, standing centre, at Trawsfynydd in 1930. Students swore that he used to follow diminutive members of his audiences along the Promenade in order to study their cranium. Ap Rhobert's engaging cartoon (*Plate 149*) confirms this widely-held view. By dint of sheer enthusiasm and commitment, however, Fleure transformed the manner in which geography was taught, and his departure to the Chair of Geography at Manchester in 1933 was a grievous blow to the College.

149

A NOTHER larger-than-life character with boundless energy was the first Director of the Welsh Plant Breeding Station and Professor of Agricultural Botany at Aberystwyth (1919–42). Affectionately known as 'Stapes', R. George Stapledon's pioneering research in grassland improvement helped to carry the name of Aberystwyth to distant corners of the earth. Stapledon was convinced that grass was a crop of vital economic importance and he, more than anyone else, showed how Welsh agriculture could strive for new standards of attainment and prosperity through the acquisition of scientific and technical knowledge. His international reputation soared when the Cahn Hill Improvement Scheme (made possible by the munificence of Sir Julian Cahn) in 1933 enabled him to carry out exhaustive surveys into hill land, experiment with new grass varieties, and improve the quality of stock. An agricultural scientist of the highest distinction, Stapledon was rewarded with an FRS and a knighthood in 1939. Following his retirement in 1942, this inspirational figure was referred to as 'British Farming's Mr Chips' (*Plate 150*).

150

SOME MEMBERS of the University staff earned distinction (for themselves if not for their Colleges) in the most unorthodox ways. At Cardiff, Professor T. Graham Brown, the first Head of the Physiology Institute opened in 1920, was a most brilliant neurophysiologist. But his heart was in climbing (*Plate 151*) and his mountaineering exploits regularly interfered with his teaching and administrative responsibilities. Matters came to a head in 1926 when a College committee was convened to discover whether there were sufficient grounds for dismissing Brown. Once Brown got wind of these developments, however, he skilfully outmanoeuvred his enemies and thwarted all attempts to engineer his dismissal. He was such a powerful and domineering figure that even after his retirement in 1947 he continued to 'squat' in his room in the department, where a specially installed camp bed and bath were just some of the amenities which made his life that much more comfortable.

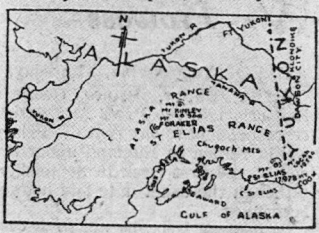

151

THE INCREASE in the number of staff was, of course, a consequence of the post-1918 boom in student numbers. Lecture rooms, quads and corridors teemed with students, many of them ex-servicemen, and, according to a Bangor correspondent, 'those silent statues on the tower have never in their existence looked down upon so many gowned forms rushing in for a "niner" or hurrying down to the cafe for cream buns and coffee'. Despite the growing numbers, each College successfully maintained a sense of corporate identity and a heart-warming *esprit de corps*. Plate 152 reveals many of the 672 students who enrolled at Bangor in 1921–2. Of these, only fifty-four came from England, one from Ireland, and twelve from abroad. In the University as a whole, student numbers had climbed to 2,850 by 1921–2, but once the large numbers of ex-servicemen had completed their studies, the normal student influx was insufficient to fill their places and a short-term slump followed until 1924–5. As the following figures reveal, total numbers reached a peak in the mid 1930s:

Year	Aberystwyth	Bangor	Cardiff	Swansea	Medical School	Total
1924–5	812	558	1019	274		2663
1934–5	828	598	1292	685	97	3500
1938–9	663	485	970	488	173	2779

By the eve of the Second World War, student numbers had declined sharply in each College, with the exception of the Medical School. At that time 92 per cent of students entering the University of Wales were born in Wales.

152

THE PRESENCE of large numbers of ex-servicemen in the Colleges after 1918 proved highly invigorating for both academic and social life. Men with scars on their minds and bodies were not prepared to be treated like children or forced to obey the puritanical code of conduct and pettifogging rules and regulations which had characterized College life before the war. 'Respectability' and 'decorum' meant nothing to them, and fossilized traditions were judged abhorrent. Nor were those who had experienced the horrors of trench warfare disposed to accept at face-value every pearl of wisdom which dropped from the lips of their tutors. Progressive ideas flourished and the call for greater freedom and responsibility became increasingly clamant. Since ex-servicemen openly flouted the armoury of restrictive regulations which College authorities deployed, a new and more relaxed atmosphere prevailed. At Aberystwyth, however, where the Nonconformist conscience was deeply embedded, male and female students were permitted to converse freely only within 'a three-mile limit' of the town (*Plate 153*), a regulation which was not abolished until 1931. D. R. Seaborne Davies, President of the Students' Representative Council at Aberystwyth in 1925, wearily confessed that 'the small clique' which governed the College 'cannot rise above the conception of a University College as a glorified County School'.

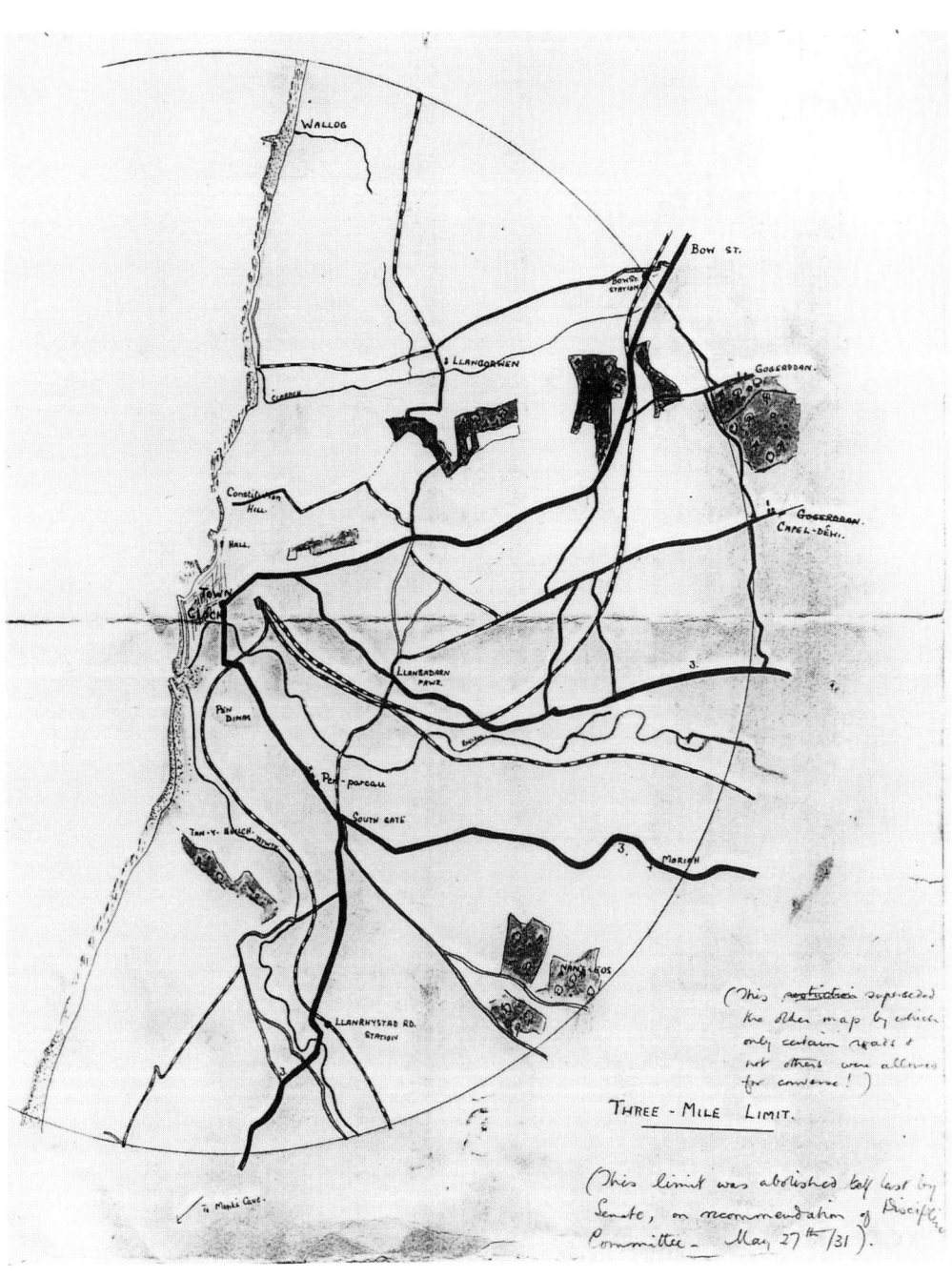

153

PATTERNS OF study and discipline in University libraries, too, changed very little, and some librarians governed their fiefdoms with a rod of iron. At Bangor, Dr Thomas Richards (*Plate 154*), a celebrated authority on Puritanism in Stuart Wales, exercised the kind of strict authority which would have earned for him the undying approval of his puritanical forebears. Appointed librarian in 1926, the legendary 'Doc Tom' used to expel noisy miscreants from the library with an explosive 'Out!' A skittish Welsh song, composed by Meredydd Evans, evoked the image of the angel Gabriel blowing the Last Trumpet and Thomas Richards declaring from his sentinel above the Top Library 'Out you go!' Another verse in *Omnibus* testifies to Tom Richards's resolute determination to enforce regulations, however antiquated:

> The noble Doctor, worthy man
> When he to rule our Libe. began
> Resolved to save, and make behave
> Those to his care confided.
> He said with stern, emphatic stress,
> 'Who wears unacademic dress,
> Or ventures in tabooed recess,
>   Must outside straight be guided
>   Must outside straight be guided.'

154

A curious silence always reigned in libraries and common rooms during 'swot fortnight' as perspiring students wrestled with their notes and their consciences (*Plate 155*). A. J. Bagnall, a research student in international politics at Aberystwyth in 1925, feared that the Welsh Colleges were becoming 'stuffy seminaries of book-worms and over-ripe scholars'! But with so many soirées, conversaziones, dances, debates, picnics and teas filling the social calendar, there were bound to be students who looked back on the past with regret and regarded the day of reckoning with considerable apprehension. A cartoon in *The Dragon* in 1920 (*Plate 156*) suggests that evading inquisitive professors, ignoring the shrill cry of alarm clocks, and making ends meet were part and parcel of a student's daily life. Joe Public, of course, as this stanza in *Omnibus* confirms, nursed the view that every student was an unemployed dimwit:

Diwaith drwy'r dydd ydyw o, – un dwl
    A gŵn du am dano;
  Yn ei boced mae baco,
  Ond dim'n ei gocoanut o.

(He's unemployed throughout the day – a dull one
    Wearing a black gown;
  Tobacco in his pocket,
  But nothing in his coconut.)

156

155

THE DAMOCLEAN sword hangs over the heads of students at the Prichard-Jones Hall in Bangor (*Plate 157*). As a correspondent in the *Western Mail* observed in June 1930: 'Freshers have been brought to realise that they have such a thing as a university number . . . and that when they enter the examination halls they need . . . their wits about them.' It was often claimed that the University was producing a surfeit of teachers and preachers, but growing numbers of students were pursuing studies in science and technology.

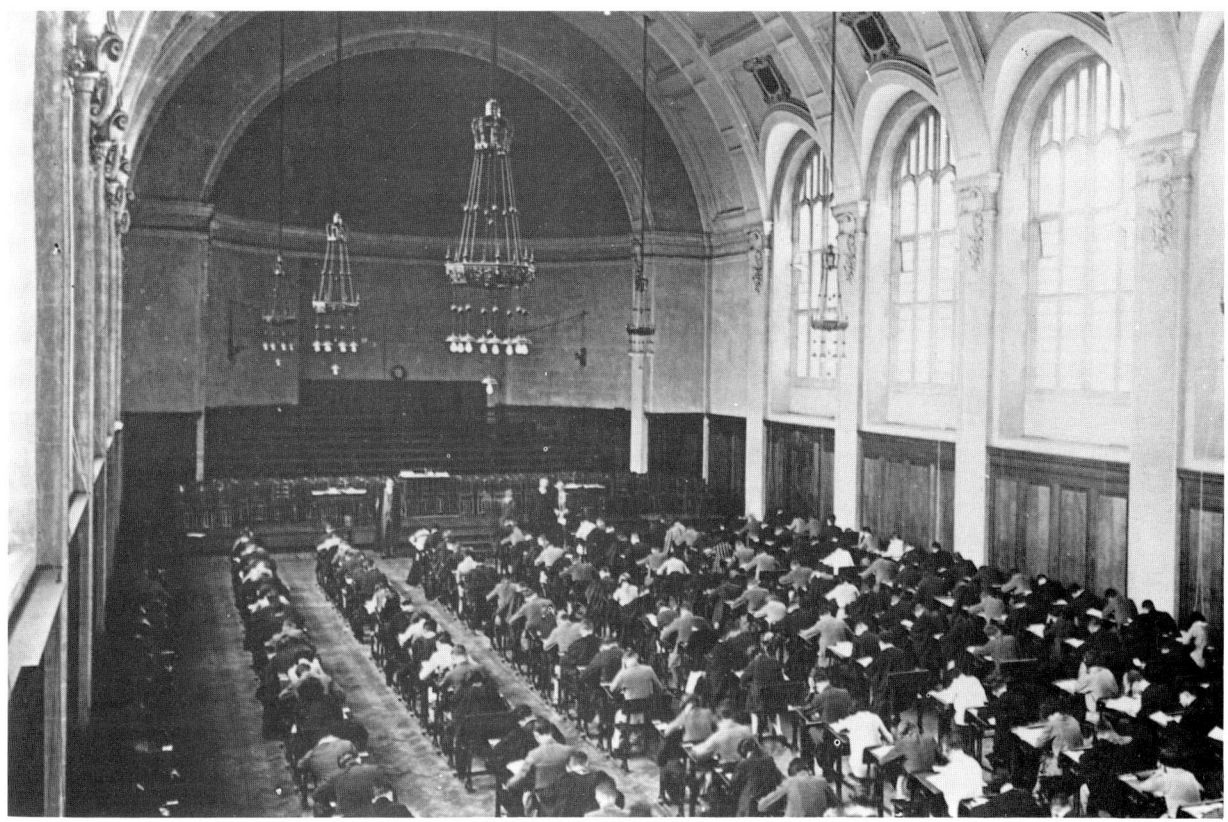

157

As far as the women students of Alexandra Hall in Aberystwyth were concerned, the trials and tribulations of examinations were as naught compared with the severe buffeting they endured during stormy winter days and nights. When news of impending storms filtered through, members of the domestic staff, aided by students, scurried to and fro, deploying sandbags and securing shutters on windows. Such precautions were often to no avail, notably in 1938. The storm of 15 January was an unforgettable experience. Terrified students huddled in their rooms as south-westerly winds and mountainous waves hurled concrete slabs into the air and demolished the front door of the Hall. A fortnight later, another horrendous tempest struck (*Plate 158*). Hurricane-force winds and thirty-foot waves left a trail of destruction along the Promenade and caused untold damage not only to College property but also to the confidence and morale of beleaguered students.

158

THE SOCIAL and cultural activities of the Colleges flourished mightily during the inter-war years, and every effort was made to strengthen inter-Collegiate relations. The Central Students' Representative Council of the University of Wales (pictured in 1920–1 in *Plate 159*) became the official representative body of the students in the constituent Colleges. Its meetings were held annually in November in each sister College in turn. The CSRC undoubtedly fostered a bond of fellowship among the Colleges since it enabled students in different parts of Wales to act in concert in matters affecting common interests. It also offered means by which recommendations from the student body could be made to the University authorities.

O. Owen (Bangor). Miss G. A. Edwards (Bangor). H. Lewis (Bangor). A. Green (Aber). T. Latham Hughes (Bangor). D. J. Williams (Aber). Miss C. Davies (Aber). A. Russell Jones (Secretary). W. T. Griffith (Cardiff).
Miss M. L. Jones (Cardiff). D. Gethin Williams (Aber). Miss A. F. Macdonald (Cardiff). E. G. Jones (President). Miss G. Walters (Aber). T. I. J. Evans (Cardiff). Miss J. Thomas (Bangor).
C. Densley F. W. Pinkara

159

160

No EVENT in the student calendar was more eagerly anticipated than the inter-collegiate week in the Lent term. For students it provided an agreeable break from academic studies and a useful means of strengthening the bonds of union between the constituent Colleges. College authorities, on the other hand, were less enthusiastic particularly when students devised ever more bizarre and annoying pranks. At Aberystwyth, for instance, lamp-posts were painted blue and green, and seats on the Promenade were tossed onto the beach. Principal Emrys Evans of Bangor, who never truly appreciated that the wicked sense of humour of high-spirited students rarely bore any malice, dubbed the occasion 'the annual plague'. It was a matter of honour for the host College that visiting rugby, soccer, hockey and netball players be accorded a riotous welcome as their trains steamed in. It was a time of warm embraces and vigorous hand-shaking. Hospitality was never found wanting and guests were paraded through the streets to the accompaniment of tin whistles, bugles and drums. Clashes on the sporting field generated great enthusiasm and encouraging telegrams, streamers, rosettes, golliwogs and teddy bears spurred on the players (*Plate 160*). 'Stick to it, Bangor' and 'Breathe on 'em Aber', cried supporters, as players keenly contested for honours.

INTER-WAR students were much more acutely conscious of their Welshness than their forebears, and from the early 1920s onwards fervently patriotic students like Idwal Jones, Iorwerth Peate, and Waldo Williams lost no opportunity to remind College authorities of their duty to protect and enhance the cultural traditions of the Welsh nation. The year 1921 was a notable one in that it witnessed the first Student Gorsedd ceremony held as part of the Inter-College Eisteddfod at Bangor (Plate 161). Needless to say, Sir John Morris-Jones, scourge of *Gorsedd Beirdd Ynys Prydain*, was conspicuous by his absence. Aberystwyth students regularly took the major honours in the inter-College eisteddfodau in the 1920s, and two of their number, bearing the improbable names 'Spivela ap Corset' and 'A Cry from the Himalayas' were admitted to the 'magic circle' in the Gorsedd ceremony at Aberystwyth in 1931 (Plate 162). On such occasions, new bards were 'initiated', usually dressed in borrowed bedsheets and gaily coloured curtains, and mock degrees were sometimes conferred. Non-Welsh-speaking students, baffled by the proceedings, disparaged such 'leprous garb'.

162

161

163

THE NAME of one jester and humorist in the early 1920s was a byword in Welsh circles. Idwal Jones entered the College at Aberystwyth in 1919 and resolved either to ignore or disobey antiquated regulations which prohibited him from addressing or escorting women students, frequenting taverns, and causing general mischief. Jones was chiefly responsible for transforming the Celtic Society into a convivial meeting where laughter reigned supreme. He composed innumerable topicals, limericks, parodies and musical comedies for the benefit of his fellow students, and wherever he and Yr Eosiaid (The Nightingales) went there was unrestrained joy and laughter (Plate 163). Indeed, the halls, rooms and corridors of the College echoed to the singing and whistling of infectious songs like 'Siani', 'Christmas is coming' and 'There's one little man left behind'. No subject was sacred, and one of Jones's most celebrated topicals was dedicated to Principal J. H. Davies, a confirmed bachelor:

If you ever see the Prinny lead him on,
With a smile so gently charming and très bon,
Take him with you when you roam
To your little country home,
Say, Papa, here am I and here is John.

When this song was first performed in public, a note of congratulation from the Principal arrived at Jones's digs the following morning. Several of this artful dodger's pranks were legendary. On one notable occasion, disguised as an aunt in a bonnet, shawl, skirt, mittens and boots, he was escorted around Carpenter Hall by the Warden and gained admittance to a study-bedroom of one of the female students.

'RAG WEEK' flourished during the inter-war years and brought colour, entertainment and noise to the streets. Students accosted passers-by with vigorously shaken collecting boxes, and medical students touched the consciences of misers by insisting that 'every penny is a bullet against disease'. In *Plate 164*, students at Cardiff enacted 'a brush with the enemy' in 1921. Facing the grim figure of Death is the conductor of a jazz-band armed with a broom-baton. In *Plate 165*, some of Bangor's students disguise themselves as David Lloyd George and his daughter Megan.

164

165

EACH COLLEGE had its own Student Rag magazine – *Ay-Yah* at Swansea, *Bang or Bust* at Bangor, *Keezle-wacka* at Aberystwyth, and *The Wail* at Cardiff. *Bang or Bust* (Plate 166) claimed a circulation of 100 million in 1933, and headlines such as 'Sextuplets at Senghennydd. Widow breaks the World Record. Three Boys. Two Girls. One Doubtful' helped to boost sales of *The Wail* in the valleys of south Wales! Substantial sums of money were also raised for local charities by a variety of ingenious stratagems like ambushes, kidnaps, bonfires and flour-bomb contests.

166

COLLEGE YELLS figured prominently in the reception organized by students for distinguished guests. When the Prince of Wales flew into Cardiff (he landed at Splott) on 21 May 1930 to open the Tatem Physics and Chemistry Laboratories, he was greeted by a deafening College Yell by Cardiff students (*Plate 167*). It ran as follows:

    Cardiffi, Cardiffi, Cardiffi!
    Cymryo! Cymryo!
    Cardiffi! Cardiffi!
    Bantahie! Bantahie!
    Nawrte! Nawrte!
    Hippory! Hippory!

The Aberystwyth Yell was reputed to be a thing of 'disciplined frightfulness'. Declaimed in a slow and deliberate manner, it made heavy demands on students wearing dentures:

Hip Hip Hoo-ray, Hip Hip Hoo-ray, Hip Hip Hoo-ray,
Boom! Whaa!! Rhaa!!! Boom! Wha!! Rha!!!
Ish Mabi! Ish Mabi!
Keezle! Keezle! Whacka! Whacka!
Keezle! Keezle! Whacka! Whacka!
Ish Mabi!
Keezle! Whacka!
Boom! Wha! Rhaa! Ph-t Hoo-ray!

Bangor's version, at least in theory, was riddled with impressive advice on dynamics:

    Hip-hip Hoorah!
    Hip-hip Hoorah!
    Hip-hip Hoorah!
    Lente Bravo Bravissimo!
      Ts s Boom Tra-ah,
      Ts s Boom Tra-ah,
    Con Spirito Sibarraboo, Sibarraboo
      Lallaballoo: Yah!
    ff Bangor Boys, Bangor Girls
      College Boys, College Girls
      Aah, Eeh, Ooh,
      Hurrah!!!

The Swansea Yell was no less demanding:

    f. Hip, Hip, Hooray.
    mf. Hip, Hip, Hooray.
    ff. Hip, Hip, Hooray.
    Staccato E-kapu-teka-teka-tay.
    Prolonged Nawrte.
    Prolonged Zzzooooump.
    Staccato Pwy sy ma, Pwy sy ma, Pwy sy ma.
    Staccato 'Tawe, 'Tawe, Abertawe.
    Staccato Hoo-ha, Derua.
    Staccato Hurrah!

In contrast, the University Yell, even in pidgin Welsh, was seldom performed:

    Pwy y'm ni
    Pwy y'm ni
    Merched Cymru, Bechgyn Cymru
    Cymru'r Wlad, Cymru'r Dref
    Cymru pob man dan y nef
    G-W-A-L-I-A
      Gwalia!!!

167

168

169

On 24–25 June 1931 a fund-raising event was held in the grounds of Cardiff Castle the like of which had not been seen in Wales since the investiture of the Prince of Wales in Caernarfon in 1911. By permission of the Marquis and Marchioness of Bute, an extraordinary fête and historical pageant attracted over 30,000 spectators (*Plates 168–9*). The whole venture, which took a nightmarish year to organize, was in aid of a new extension to the Students' Union Building in Park Place as a memorial to students of the College who had fallen during the First World War. The *primum mobile* was the Principal J. F. Rees (*Plate 170*) whose wife, a heroic lady, rallied the wives of the academic staff and kept their spirits high in spite of stormy committee meetings and chaotic rehearsals. The highlight of the proceedings was a picturesque (and often bizarre) enactment by costumed staff, students and schoolchildren of five major episodes in the history of Cardiff. Just about everyone, from the Principal (who filled the part of Ralph, Archdeacon of Llandaff) to the Head Porter, was dragooned into dressing up as Romans or Vikings or Normans (*Plate 171*). Surrounding mail-clad knights, rustic peasants and nubile maidens were hoopla stalls, bran tubs, coconut shies, and Madame Marie, a well-known palmist, while the National Orchestra of Wales, the Park and Dare Workmen's Silver Band, and the College Madrigal Singers provided musical accompaniment. The event was a colossal, but thoroughly worthwhile, event, for the princely sum of £4,050 was raised.

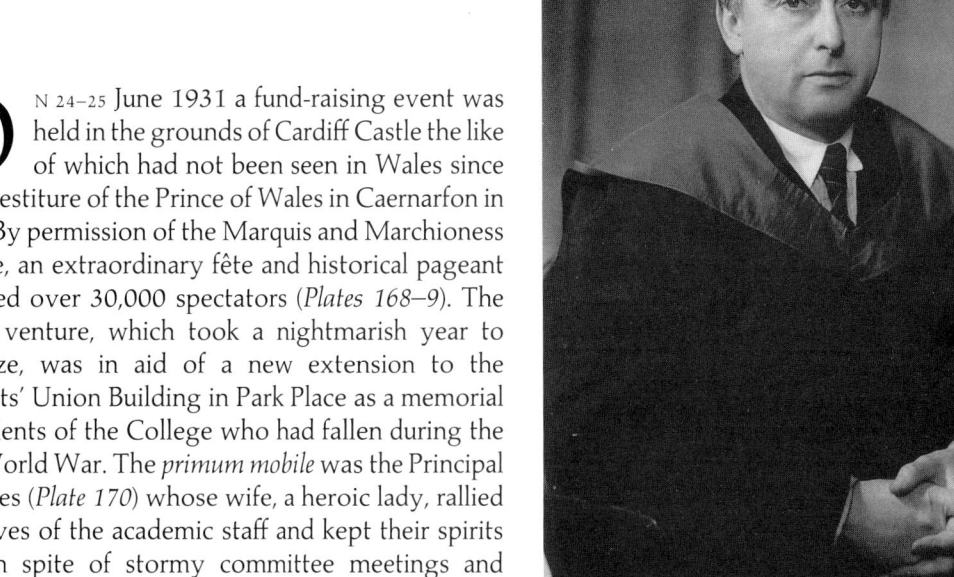

170

171

LIGHT-HEARTED hoaxes, pranks and leg-pulls were part and parcel of student life in the inter-war years. Gullible freshers were lured into bogus examinations, statues of eminent men were whitewashed, and visiting guests were made to run the gauntlet of unofficial 'welcoming parties'. What the *Cambrian News* called 'a real Welsh welcome' was conferred upon the unsuspecting Sir Austen Chamberlain when he visited Aberystwyth on 12 February 1932 to deliver his presidential address to the Debating Union. When he stepped from the train he was confronted by an 'army' of students, many of them wearing monocles. Others were dressed as seaside landladies and carrying brooms. Apparently, the officials of the Students' Debates Union had been kidnapped and locked in one of the College boathouses. The bogus officials duly escorted Sir Austen to the town workhouse which was described to him as a 'home for broken-down professors'. Once he had recovered his composure, Chamberlain proceeded to the College to deliver his lecture on 'The Lessons of Locarno' (Plate 172).

173

A MONG THE most mysterious and bizarre rites which commended themselves to students were mock funerals. Students were acutely conscious of the traditions of their respective Colleges and were deeply attached to their places of study. It was entirely fitting, therefore, that the students of Bangor, at the time of the closure of the much-loved but hopelessly inadequate Penrhyn Arms in 1932, should have interred and laid to rest an effigy of their old habitation in full public view (*Plates 173–4*).

174

COLLEGE Principals were quite properly deemed fair game by cartoonists, and lampoons were especially rife during Rag Week. This cartoon (*Plate 175*), published in *Omnibus* in 1933, captures Reichel's successor at Bangor. Sir D. Emrys Evans, a former student and past President of the Students' Representative Council, was the first graduate of the University of Wales to become Principal of one of its constituent Colleges. In 1953 the University celebrated its sixtieth anniversary by publishing Sir Emrys's volume *The University of Wales. A Historical Sketch*, a work which, like its author, was informative, elegant and wise. Even so, his study was essentially history written from the administrator's eyrie, and not a few innocent readers wondered whether students had ever figured in the University of Wales.

175

INTER-COLLEGIATE clashes on the rugby field continued to draw large and enthusiastic crowds of supporters. Aberystwyth ruled the roost in the 1920s, taking full advantage of the seemingly inexhaustible supply of talented young players from 'fly-half factories' in the valleys of south Wales. The galaxy of talent at its disposal enabled the College to win the University of Wales and the British Universities' Championship in 1927–8 (Plate 176). Bangor, too, emerged from the doldrums and, egged

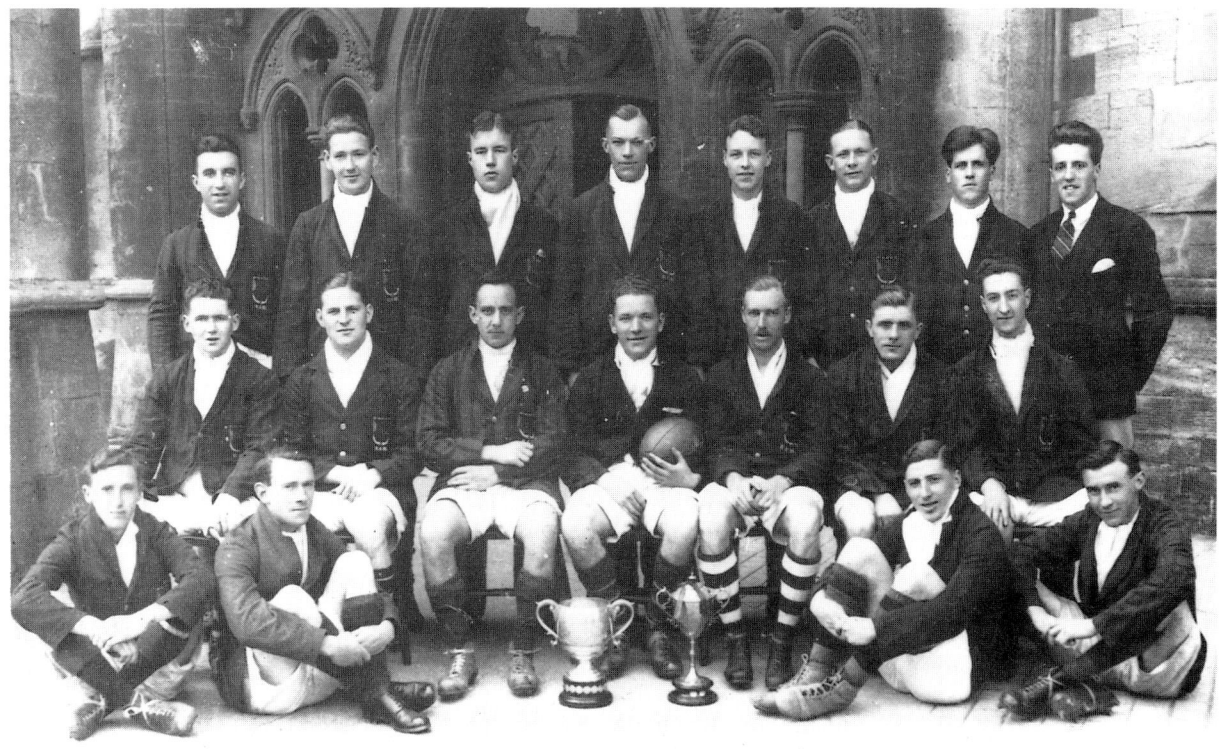

176

177

on by the President of the Rugby Club, the irrepressible Professor R. L. Archer, the team lost on one occasion only in the 1925–6 season and delighted its supporters by vanquishing powerful sides like Liverpool and Manchester (*Plate 177*). It was Swansea, however, which proved the major breeding-ground for international players. The team which convincingly defeated Cardiff in January 1929 (*Plate 178*) included three future captains of Wales: the massive Watcyn Thomas (fifth from the left in the rear), the bone-crunching tackler Claude Davey (extreme left in front row) and the elusive runner Idwal Rees (second from left in front row). Third from the left in the middle row is T. J. Morgan, the scholar and essayist who became Registrar of the University of Wales in 1951.

178

By 1924–5 Aberystwyth College possessed one of the most progressive and successful amateur soccer teams in Wales. Inspired by E. R. (Ned) Harries, a dogged and never-say-die half-back, the College team swept aside Bangor, Cardiff, Swansea, Bristol and Liverpool in its successful quest for the British Universities' Championship (*Plate 179*).

In contrast, Bangor's team was long on enthusiasm and short on natural ability. Even impartial observers confirmed that Aberystwyth might have scored many more than six goals against Bangor in the inter-Collegiate match in 1924. Not unexpectedly, perhaps, contests between them were ill-tempered affrays, with much elbowing and ankle-tapping.

179

According to an earnest correspondent in the student magazine *Omnibus* in 1935, boxing was a most 'desirable sport' because it developed 'those physical and moral qualities which are essential to success in life'. Of all people, he continued, 'the most liable to become soft and effeminate' was the male student. His views were not widely shared, however, and the Boxing Club at Aberystwyth (*Plate 180*) was temporarily disbanded following widespread criticism in the mid 1930s.

180

IT WOULD be wrong to suppose that students were simply concerned with parochial issues and were unwilling to embroil themselves in international affairs. In the 1930s fruitful links were established with universities in Europe and there is no doubt that the implications of the rise of Fascism were keenly felt. Invitations were issued to eminent politicians, social reformers, and musicians. In January 1937 Luigi Gasparini – 'the Kreisler of the cello' – enchanted his audience during a recital organized by the Dante Alighieri Society in the Drapers' Library at Cardiff (*Plates 181–2*). At Aberystwyth an International

181

182

Relations Club and a Cosmopolitan Club prospered, not least because their members were determined to discuss international problems in an objective and non-partisan manner. In 1941 Jan Masaryk, son of Thomas, the founder and first President of Czechoslovakia, delivered an inspiring address to the Debates Union at Aberystwyth (*Plate 183*), during which he seized the opportunity to remind students that Czechoslovakia was 'a country and not a contagious disease' and that 'if the other side wins, another Stone Age will descend for centuries on tortured humanity'. In 1943 Aberystwyth students established the Masaryk Society, with the avowed aim of fostering international fellowship.

183

WHEN THE Second World War broke out in 1939, students knuckled down to their academic tasks with uncommon diligence. Surprised and delighted tutors observed that many of their pupils had never worked harder in their lives. Thanks to the energy and commitment of staff and students, an air of normality was maintained. As had been the case in the Great War, it was business as usual. None the less, the war brought changes in routine, teaching and atmosphere. Degree courses were shortened and several postgraduate schemes of research were abandoned. The shortage of paper supplies and dwindling numbers of students meant that student magazines were slimmer and, save for spirited cartoons like that published in *The Wail* at Cardiff in *Plate 184*, rather more sombre in tone. Much College ritual was abandoned and restrictions were placed on social activities and recreational programmes. No College took its responsibilities more seriously than Bangor. The Prichard-Jones Hall, together with cellars and basements, were commandeered, the 'Main Corridor' was evacuated, and 10,000 sandbags, treated with Cuprinol, were placed at the ready. Such precautions provoked great resentment among students, all the more so when the College Senate prohibited students from selling political newspapers such as *The Daily Worker*, the *Welsh Nationalist* and *Peace News*. The editor of *Omnibus* launched a scathing attack on 'officious, pettifogging, pocket dictators' who made life even more miserable than Hitler's forces promised.

184

COLLEGE students and members of staff enrolled in units of the Home Guard, the Air Training Squadron and contingents of the Officers' Training Corps, and courses were arranged on fire-fighting, first-aid and anti-gas protection. Compulsory fire-watching was introduced in 1940 and, as the page drawn from the log book of fire-watchers at the University Registry reveals (Plate 185), long periods of monotony were punctuated by short, sharp bursts of sirens, gunfire and bombing. The College at Cardiff suffered severely at the hands of the *Luftwaffe*, notably on 26 February 1941 when five high-explosive bombs caused extensive damage to academic buildings and killed a student who was fulfilling his duties as a fire-watcher. In the same month, students at Swansea were terrified when, during 'the Three Nights' Blitz', thousands of high-explosive and incendiary bombs dropped by the *Luftlotte* (Airfleet) 3 virtually wiped out all major landmarks in the town centre. Mercifully, Aberystwyth and Bangor were spared much of the misery caused by bombs, shrapnel and fires, and the dislocation was less than might have been expected. It was also reassuring to discover that war time conditions could uncover hidden talents: Professor H. H. Rowley, a Hebrew scholar at Bangor, revealed a curious and hitherto unsuspected aptitude for working stirrup-pumps and defusing incendiary bombs.

As this cartoon in *The Dragon* suggests (*Plate 186*), growing numbers of able-bodied students enlisted in the armed forces and, as a result, student numbers declined appreciably. The number of full-time students fell from 2,779 in 1938–9 to 2,132 in 1943–4. In difficult circumstances members of staff did their best to fulfil their academic obligations and maintain normal services. Courses of lectures were arranged for troops stationed locally and many intrepid tutors braved the black-out in order to travel to military camps to deliver talks on current affairs, economics, history and literature. Students, too, were obliged to improvise and adapt. The inter-Collegiate eisteddfod became a much smaller and quieter event, and the rationing of food and petrol led to the cancellation of long-standing recreational fixtures. Sports teams lost many of their ablest players to the armed forces, and an enforced diet of spam and powdered-egg omelettes failed to improve the performance of those who stayed behind. At Cardiff, makeshift rugby teams were fashioned from among the three 'Ms' – miners, medicals and ministerials – and, according to W. B. Cleaver, the ministerial students invariably caused mayhem, the medicals blanched whenever blood flowed, and the miners fared least well on muddy waterlogged pitches!

"The rest of my Honours Class has been called up."

186

LIKE OTHER universities in Britain, the University of Wales was obliged to admit refugee students from Europe, and their numbers were further swollen by evacuated students and staff from the London Colleges. For the most part, these 'migrants' settled down swiftly and brought enthusiasm and freshness to academic study and student life. Around 200 students from University College, London, and Westminster College were entertained at Bangor (*Plate 187*), and although a minority of them were derisive of Welsh customs and traditions, the bulk of the 'evacuees' were eager to collaborate closely and happily with their hosts. Welsh Colleges were believed to be less vulnerable to aerial assaults than the London Colleges though, by a curious quirk of fortune, the buildings which students of the School of Pharmacy and the King's College for Women had vacated suffered less damage than that which befell their new 'home' in Cardiff.

187

THE INFLUX of substantial numbers of students from London taxed the ingenuity of accommodation officers at Bangor, and Orson Wood, a science tutor, was obliged to set up a temporary laboratory in a bicycle shop in the High Street (*Plate 188*). In each of the Colleges members of staff were determined to produce skilled men and women who would not only help to meet the challenge of war but also be equipped to play their part in the reconstruction of society in peacetime.

188

MUSIC AND song were also unifying forces during the trying years of war. Welsh was still very much the principal language among students at Bangor and within the small, close-knit student community *nosweithiau llawen*, concerts and eisteddfodau helped to brighten the gloom which generally prevailed in wartime. Abundant talent was available, but the entertainers *par excellence* from 1943 onwards were *Triawd y Coleg* (the College Trio) (*Plate 189*). Local concert halls were filled to overflowing whenever the gifted trio of Robin Williams (left), Cledwyn Jones (centre) and Meredydd Evans (right), accompanied on the piano by Maimie Noel Jones and Ffrancon Thomas, regaled audiences with popular songs like 'Hen Feic Penny Farthing fy Nhaid', 'Pictiwrs Bach y Borth' and 'Cabinet F'Ewyrth John'.

189

ALTHOUGH conscription threw recreational pursuits into confusion, students were determined never to permit wartime privations to dull their enthusiasm. London students brought new life into sporting contests and teams representing the Army and the RAF provided exacting opposition for scratch College sides. One happy (though sometimes over-vigorous) event, begun in 1940, was the annual football match between the University students at Bangor and the Normal College. *Plate 190* shows the victorious University XI with the coveted Woolworth Cup in 1945–6. Among the budding luminaries are Meredydd Evans (standing, second left) and Cledwyn Jones (seated, third right) both members of the celebrated 'Triawd y Coleg'. Aled Eames, who subsequently made his mark as a historian of seafaring in Wales, is the goalkeeper.

190

As the war drew to its conclusion there was much rejoicing in the University of Wales when, in 1944, Thomas Jones (known to all and sundry as TJ) was unanimously elected President of the University College of Wales, Aberystwyth (*Plate 191*). Born in Rhymney in 1870, TJ had entered the College at Aberystwyth in 1920, and in his address to the Literary and Debating Society in 1945 he informed the students: 'Our Welsh Colleges are such recent foundations that I can boast that I am older than all of them!' Even though his *Alma Mater* had spurned a golden opportunity to appoint him Principal in 1919, TJ bore no grudges, for Aberystwyth always had first claim on his loyalty and seldom did the College apply in vain for his assistance. As Deputy Secretary to the Cabinet under four prime ministers, he was ideally placed to advance the interests of the College and the University as a whole. Indeed, Principal Goronwy Rees subsequently (and rather uncharitably) referred to him as 'a kind of *éminence grise* in the management of the Welsh people'. At any rate, TJ brought enormous authority and prestige to the office of President and, as E. L. Ellis has observed, he remained until his death in 1955 the 'embodiment of the old, proud tag: "Once an Aber man, always an Aber man"'.

191

TONGUES wagged freely in academic circles and beyond when, in 1943, W. J. Gruffydd, Professor of Welsh at Cardiff (1918–46) (*Plate 192*), was persuaded (chiefly by Thomas Jones, who was determined to slay the nationalist dragon) to stand as the Liberal parliamentary candidate for the constituency of the University of Wales, a seat which had been created in 1918. His great adversary, Saunders Lewis, had already been declared the Plaid Cymru candidate, but Welsh nationalism had been deeply tainted by Nazism and Gruffydd won the seat comfortably. He was re-elected in 1945 and remained the sitting member until university seats were abolished in 1950. The son of a Caernarfonshire quarryman, Gruffydd was an eminent poet, critic and scholar. *Y Llenor*, the celebrated quarterly periodical which he edited from 1922 to 1951, was as widely read for his hard-hitting editorial columns as for its literary content. A gruff, opinionated, pugnacious man, Gruffydd relished controversy. As one of his students observed: 'We watched him often, preparing for a tournament like a knight in the age of chivalry ... *Gruffyddus contra mundum*.' One of his colleagues at Cardiff noticed that he 'wore the look of a surly tortoise' whenever he was obliged to address a dull or uncongenial class of students. His enemies in staff common rooms throughout the University were legion: 'that damned Gruffydd' was a common observation.

192

THE WAR, with its massive bloodshed and destruction, left its mark on students for many years after 1945. As was the case following the First World War, ex-servicemen who returned to Welsh Colleges were by no means docile, pliant creatures. When Emanuel Shinwell, War Minister in the Labour Government, came to Aberystwyth in February 1949 to recruit for the army, former soldiers in the student ranks were appalled by his arrogance. 'You may not be disciplined now', cried Shinwell, 'but you will be when we get hold of you.' A large and noisy demonstration followed, during which students displayed banners bearing mock slogans like 'Join Fred Karno's Army' and 'Drop the Atom Bomb now – on the Pentagon', and heckled Shinwell unmercifully (*Plate 193*). Incensed by such 'hooligan' behaviour, the *Cambrian News* voiced its fervent hope that the reception given to Shinwell would not create a false impression of Aberystwyth as a 'hot-bed of pacifism, nationalism or any other 'ism'.

193

When the Duke of Kent died in 1942, the office of Chancellor remained vacant until 1 May 1948 when His Royal Highness the Duke of Edinburgh and Earl of Merioneth was elected by the University Court. *Plate 194* reveals the Installation Ceremony in the spacious Prichard-Jones Hall, Bangor, on 28 April 1949, when the new Chancellor received the degree of Doctor in Legibus, *honoris causa*, from the Vice-Chancellor, Principal D. Emrys Evans. His first act as Chancellor was to confer the honorary degree of Doctor of Music on the Princess Elizabeth. During the ensuing luncheon, the Duke admitted that he had never been to a university before, but now found himself Chancellor, and that he had never worked for a degree, but now found himself with the much easier task of giving them away! The Duke (later The Prince Philip) remained 'Head and Chief Officer' of the University until 1976. These were to prove years of momentous importance for the nature of the University of Wales.

194

THE MAGIC words on the lips of university principals in the post-1945 era were 'rebuilding' and 'reconstruction'. As the pressure to increase the student intake became irresistible, major new building schemes were launched in each of the Welsh Colleges. Striking developments occurred at Aberystwyth, where much of the College was relocated, at Swansea, where a magnificent new campus was built on the western side of the Singleton site, and at Cardiff, where the Welsh National School of Medicine was rehoused. Even as early as 1929 Principal Henry Stuart Jones had dreamed of building 'an Athens fair in Ceredigion's pleasant land', for in that year Joseph Davies-Bryan, a former student who had opened drapers' stores in the Near East and earned the nickname 'the Selfridge of Egypt', had donated to the College at Aberystwyth an extensive site of eighty-five acres on the Penglais estate for the erection of new college buildings. In 1936 Percy Thomas (later Sir Percy) and Son prepared a detailed survey of the site and submitted a handsome building scheme which incorporated academic and residential accommodation (*Plate 195*). Progress in the building programme, however, was interrupted by the Second World War, and even when D. Alban Davies, a former milk merchant in London, generously donated a further 220 acres on the Penglais site, major building plans were delayed until the 1960s.

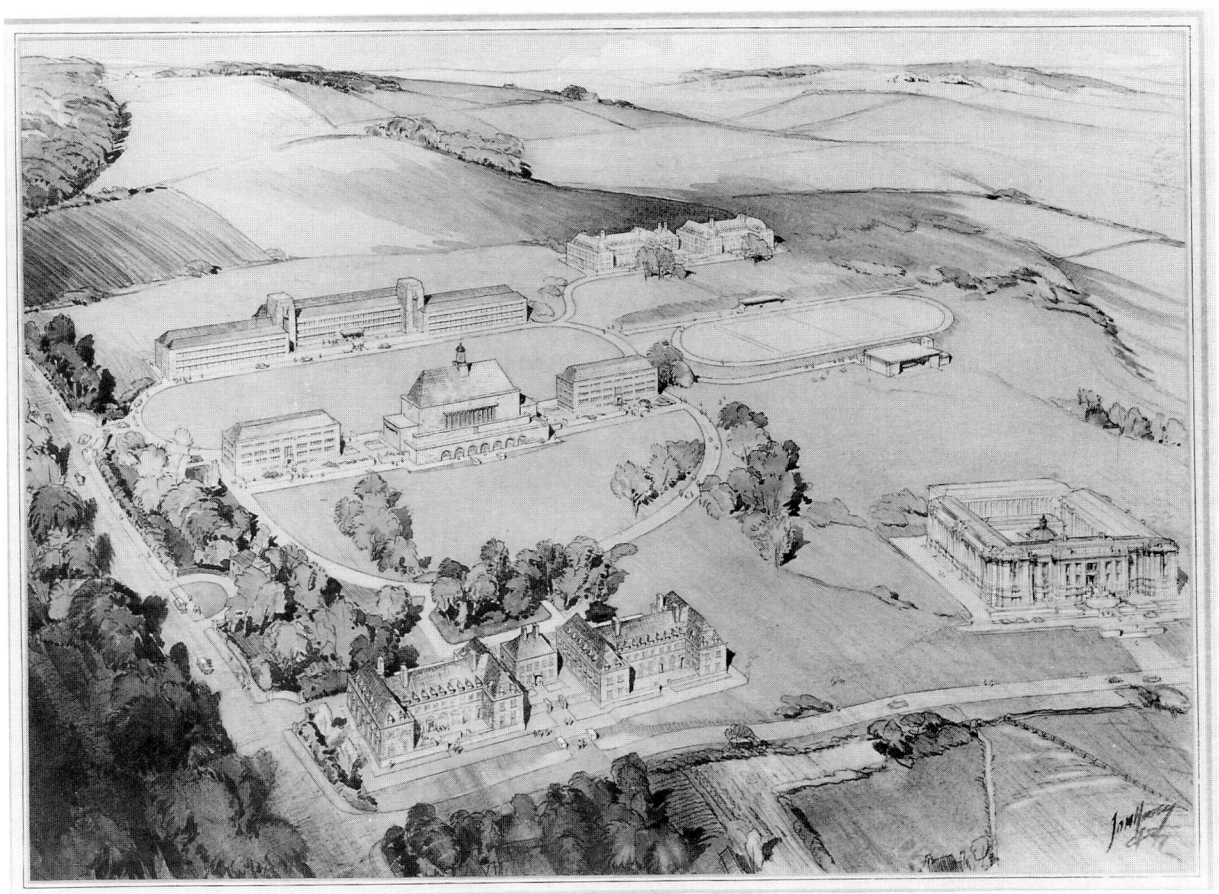

195

MEANWHILE, the relatively placid atmosphere of university life at Aberystwyth in the 1950s was rudely disturbed in 1956–7 by a *cause célèbre* involving Principal Goronwy Rees. Although born in Aberystwyth and the son of a highly respected Nonconformist minister, the Oxford-educated Rees had been ill at ease in his native town ever since his appointment in 1953. His unorthodox life-style rendered him suspect in the eyes of staid administrators and chapel deacons, and his widely publicized contempt for Welsh nationalism, together with his belief that the Welsh language was a stifling burden, did not endear him to Welsh-speaking academics or local people. Nevertheless, Rees was a handsome and outstandingly gifted man who, according to *The Courier*, 'created an arresting first impression'. Students adored him and whenever he addressed them at meetings he was assured an ovation and a rousing rendition of 'For he's a jolly good fellow'. His position as Principal, however, became untenable when he published a series of sensational articles in *The People*, exposing Guy Burgess (a close friend of his at Oxford in the 1930s) as a drunken, homosexual Comintern agent. The 'establishment' at Aberystwyth (later described by Rees as 'a theocratic society, ruled by priests and elders') was outraged. A Committee of Inquiry was swiftly established, but before its conclusions were presented to the Council Rees tendered his resignation (*Plate 196*). This distressing episode provoked considerable bitterness in both town and College. Despite the highly partisan account of the affair which Rees subsequently published in his brilliant autobiographical work, *A Chapter of Accidents* (1972), it is hard to avoid the conclusion that he was the architect of his own downfall.

196

197

G ORONWY Rees's successor in 1958 was Sir Thomas Parry (he was knighted in 1978) (*Plate 197*), whose much acclaimed study of the poetry of Dafydd ap Gwilym in 1952 had established his reputation as a scholar and critic. Although Parry was sensible of the historical significance of 'the College by the Sea' and the sentimental attachment to it, he preferred not to dwell too much on the past. He saw very clearly that the future of the College lay on the Penglais site and, under his wise leadership, large-scale changes were set in motion. Indeed, by 1967 (*Plate 198*), Aberystwyth had virtually been transformed into 'the College on the Hill'. Grandiose building schemes, financed by substantial government grants and handsome donations from well-wishers, enabled the College to erect new buildings for Biology, Physical Sciences, the Faculty of Economic and Social Studies, the Faculty of Law, Geography, Geology, and Rural Science, as well as student halls of residence.

198

FURTHER building plans on the Penglais site were designed to maximize the potential of the sloping nature of the site and to serve the needs of the community as well as the College. The new focal point of the campus became the Great Hall and the Students' Union building (*Plate 199*), completed in 1970 and officially opened by Lord Morris of Borth-y-Gest in April 1971. The Great Hall, Bell Tower and Concourse area gained prestigious awards from the Civic Trust, the Royal Institute of British Architects, and the National Eisteddfod of Wales. A year later, the College Theatre – Theatr y Werin – was opened, and this was followed by a major new Arts block which was appropriately named 'The Hugh Owen Building'. These were years of highly significant growth and development within the College.

199

AT SWANSEA, too, major new building schemes, designed primarily to advance the interests of science and technology, were launched. A crucial turning-point was the appointment of John Scott Fulton, Jowett Fellow and Tutor in Politics at Balliol College, Oxford, to the office of Principal in 1947 (*Plate 200*). Fulton was not only a shrewd policy-maker and administrator, but also an extremely hard taskmaster. His energy, resourcefulness in debate, and great foresight made him the very man to maximize the opportunities which presented themselves. He immediately set about winning public approval for major rebuilding plans, and proved conspicuously successful in wooing the support of local councillors and in improving town-gown relations, so much so that in December 1950 Swansea Corporation generously donated to the College twenty-seven acres of parkland on the western side of Singleton Abbey. This magnificent site was immediately earmarked for a programme of exceptional expansion (*Plate 201*). By 1958 a development plan had been designed by Sir

200

201

Percy Thomas and Son (*Plate 202*), a firm whose reputation had soared in the wake of its attractive scheme for the Penglais site at Aberystwyth. The focal point of the new campus would be College House (which was opened in 1962 and much later re-christened Fulton House), which was designed to contain a refectory, dining and common rooms, bars, a bank, a post office, and a medical centre. Surrounding this pivotal building would be modern residential accommodation and buildings for teaching and research. By the time Principal Fulton left, in 1959, to become Vice-Chancellor of the newly established University of Sussex, he had successfully established the foundations of the College's expansion. In September 1960 the College Development Fund Appeal set itself a target sum of £500,000. Expenditure on building projects was considerable, and the authorities at Swansea were obliged to revise, adjust and hasten their building programmes in order to cater for growing numbers of students. Building contractors noisily demolished old buildings, cleared new sites, and eventually erected a handsome new campus which cost over £7 million (*Plate 203*).

202

203

THE THIRD institution to witness radical changes in its location and character was the Welsh National School of Medicine. During the post-war years it became evident that facilities at its headquarters in Newport Road, adjacent to the Royal Infirmary, were hopelessly inadequate and a serious obstacle to effective medical education. As student numbers expanded swiftly, authorities at the Medical School made their concern clear. The only practical solution seemed to be the erection of a new teaching centre on the outskirts of Cardiff. Public speculation as to where that precise location might be was satisfied when, in 1950, Cardiff City Corporation sold to the Ministry of Health a 53-acre site on the Heath Estate, a mile from the city centre. Lack of capital for a massive building programme, however, meant that there were no quick and easy answers to accommodation problems in Newport Road. Negotiations dragged on and, in such uncertain circumstances, it was an act of faith to invite leading architects to submit proposals for a Medical Teaching Centre comprising a Teaching Hospital, a Medical School, a Dental Hospital and a Dental School. The successful plan (*Plate 204*), submitted and approved in 1960, was designed by S. W. Milburn and Partners, in association with M. Harding and J. Surtees. In 1965 the first phase of the scheme at Heath Park was completed when the Dental School and Hospital

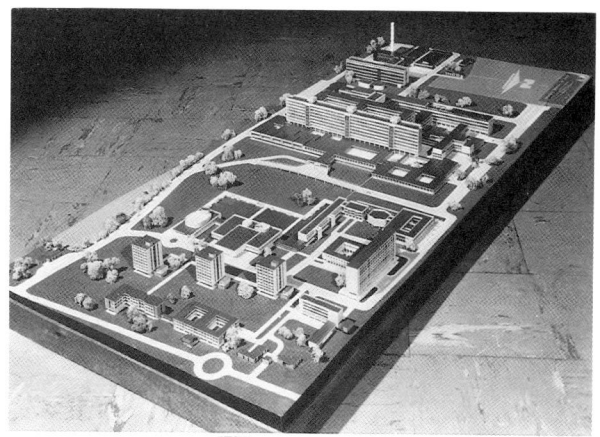

204

were opened, swiftly followed a year later by the Tenovus Institute for Cancer Research. In November 1971 Queen Elizabeth II was invited to open the University Hospital of Wales, an 800-bedded hospital with a fully integrated Clinical Medical School (*Plate 205*). In July 1984 the Welsh National School of Medicine was granted a Royal Charter which not only gave long overdue recognition to the institution as an international centre of excellence, but also enabled it to become known as the University of Wales College of Medicine.

205

ONE OF the consequences of the expansion in higher education was an opportunity for the University of Wales to admit new colleges into its fold for the first time since 1920. The Robbins Report of 1963 recommended that Colleges of Advanced Technology be elevated into universities, and on 19 April 1968 Sir Cennydd Traherne, Lord Lieutenant of Glamorgan, presented the Royal Charter granted to the University of Wales Institute of Science and Technology to HRH the Duke of Edinburgh, Chancellor of the University of Wales (*Plate 206*) who, in turn, presented it to Dr Alexander Harvey, Principal of the new University College. Grateful students at UWIST placed a wry advert in *The Times* when news of the award of the charter was first made public: 'University of Wales – on November 14, 1967, in London, a son (UWIST). Grateful thanks to all concerned.' Having made the transition from CAT to university, UWIST addressed itself to the task of establishing the closest possible links with the world of industry, commerce and science, and in offering attractive vocational training to budding technocrats.

206

207

IN 1971 St David's College, Lampeter, was incorporated as a constituent institution of the University of Wales, with the status of a School (Plate 207). Nestling in the heart of rural mid Wales, this neo-Gothic building, imaginatively designed by the architect C. R. Cockerell, was the oldest College in Wales. Its foundation stone had been laid by Dr Thomas Burgess, Bishop of St David's, as early as 1822, and the College itself opened in 1827. In 1852 (BD) and 1865 (BA), it was empowered to award its own degrees and to admit students without religious test. When the possibility of establishing a university in Wales was discussed, Lampeter was heavily involved in the negotiations, only to discover, in the upshot, that the door was firmly closed in its face on the grounds that its sectarian nature made it a radically different institution from the other three secular Colleges. This rebuff left a legacy of bitterness and henceforth Lampeter's relations with the University of Wales were, as Sir Emrys Evans remarked, 'rather like those of a moth to the flame – an alternation of darts and retreats as its wings were threatened with singeing'. It continued to nurse hopes of becoming a fully-fledged university college and it struggled heroically to secure Treasury aid and

208

161

admission into the University of Wales. That this ambition was realized owed much to the resolution of John Roland Lloyd Thomas (*Plate 208*), Principal of the College from 1953 to 1975, whose volume *Moth or Phoenix* (1980) provides a spirited account of Lampeter's quest for parity. As befitted a man who had seen overseas service in Italy and Tunisia, Principal Lloyd Thomas's account was riddled with military metaphors and combative chapter-headings such as 'Arrival and first recce. Battle stations', 'Minor skirmishings' and 'Final Solution'. The case was vigorously argued and won. On 24 May 1971 a new Supplemental Charter was sealed, thereby enabling the College to enter the University of Wales, as a Constituent School, bearing the title St David's University College. In 1988 it acquired full College status.

209

NOT LEAST among the newcomers to the expanding University of Wales was a residential educational centre, pleasantly located in wooded parkland five miles north of Newtown in mid Wales. In May 1960 Miss Margaret Davies, the Welsh benefactress, generously donated Gregynog Hall and an estate of 750 acres, together with an annual endowment of £12,000 for its upkeep, to the University (*Plate 209*). The Hall was first occupied by the University in September 1963 and it opened its doors to study groups, short courses and conferences in the 1964–5 session. Since then it has grown and flourished mightily as a focal point for the cultural life of mid Wales and as an extremely congenial venue for a wide range of staff colloquia and student courses. For many undergraduates from the constituent Colleges, the annual visit to Gregynog is a major highlight in the academic and social calendar. Not least among the successes of Gregynog is its Press – Gwasg Gregynog – a limited company established in 1978 and owned by the University – which publishes a diverse list of exquisitely bound printed books (*Plate 210*).

4 CERDDI ROBERT WILLIAMS PARRY

Robert Williams Parry, *Cerddi Robert Williams Parry* [Poems]. Selected and edited with an introduction and notes by Thomas Parry. xiv + 113pp. 282 x 175mm. ILLUSTRATION: Six wood engravings by Peter Reddick. Calligraphic title-page, poem titles and Press device by Ieuan Rees. PRINTING: On the Soldans; the title-page and poem titles in brown and green, the device in green. TYPE: Hand-set in 14pt Baskerville. EDITION: 245 copies on hand-made paper specially manufactured by Wookey Hole Mill. BINDING: *Ordinary*. Copies 1 to 200 and 30 un-numbered copies bound in quarter green goatskin, blind rule, with green buckram boards, the title blind embossed on upper cover and titled in gold on the spine. Copies 1 to 143 bound by Sangorski & Sutcliffe, subsequent copies by James Brockman. Published in December at £112. *Special*. Copies 1 to XV bound by Sydney Cockerell, to a design by Joan Rix Tebbutt, in green goatskin with a flower pattern tooled in blind and gold on upper cover and green leather label on the spine, hand-made paper doublures, green leather joints. Issued in early 1981 at £350. A green buckram felt-lined solander box, with green leather label on the spine, made by Desmond Shaw was offered as an extra at £25.

210

REMARKABLE advances in building programmes within the University of Wales were, of course, the direct result of appreciable expansion in student numbers. From 1938–9 to 1958–9, when this photograph of a demure fresher arriving at Bangor was taken (*Plate 211*), the total number of full-time students in the University of Wales increased by 110 per cent. In 1946–7 the total number of students – 4,071 – was higher than at any other time in the history of the University, and this considerable influx of mostly ex-servicemen placed a heavy strain on the resources of the Colleges. But from 1946 onwards financial support from the University Grants Committee constituted the major part of the income of the Colleges and this inevitably led to an upward trend in student numbers. By 1959–60 there were 6,159 students in full-time education in the University of Wales. Even so, to the public at large, universities still appeared elitist and complacent institutions, engaged in 'non-productive' teaching and research, and reluctant to open their doors to working-class students.

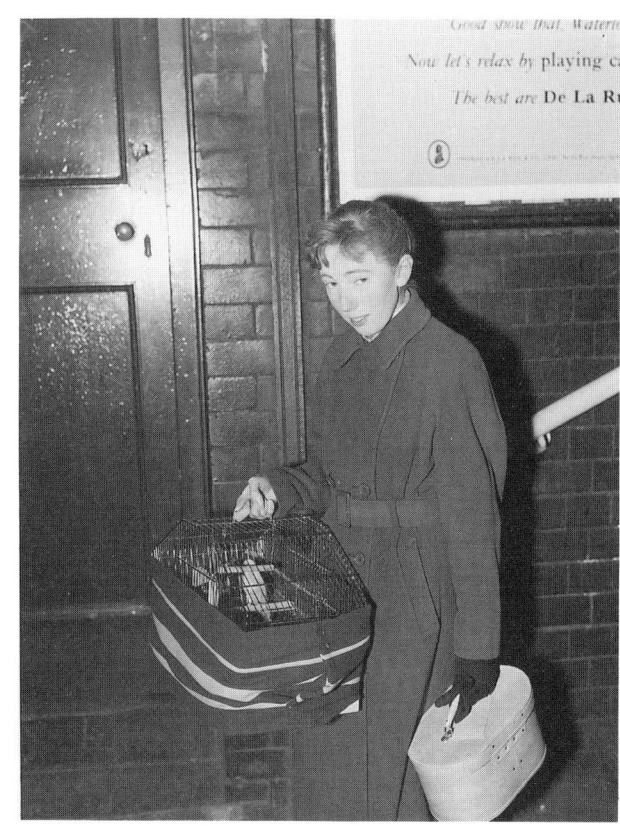

211

THE PRESSURE to increase the size of Welsh Colleges became irresistible when the celebrated Robbins Report was published in October 1963. The overwhelming thrust of the Report was that universities should no longer cater for a minority interest – epitomized by this dashing student at Bangor in the late 1950s (*Plate 212*) – but that a place in full-time education be granted to all who were qualified to receive it and anxious to do so. The Report's recommendation that the universities should house around 350,000 students by 1980–1 was met in some quarters with much incredulity and wringing of hands. Kingsley Amis's celebrated dictum – 'more means worse' – was widely publicized. However, the authorities at each of the Welsh Colleges firmly endorsed 'the Robbins Principle' and the numbers game began to dominate policy-making. Student numbers rose swiftly, and in fact more than doubled between 1962–3 (7,618) and 1972–3 (15,469). By any standards, this was an astonishing development and it undoubtedly ushered in substantial changes in the nature of social and academic life in the constituent Colleges of the University of Wales.

212

IN HIS report to the Court of Governors at Aberystwyth in 1963, Principal Thomas Parry paid a glowing tribute to the University of Wales for its distinctive contribution to the education of first generation students: 'Those of us in this room who are the sons and daughters of small farmers, farm servants, miners, steelworkers, quarrymen and shopkeepers might very well never have gone to a university, had we been born in England.' Many such students subsequently achieved fame in all walks of life. In 1950 Carwyn Rees James, a miner's son from Cefneithin, graduated with honours in Welsh at Aberystwyth (*Plate 213*). He captained the College rugby side and, according to *The Dragon*, was 'a born footballer whom one does not hesitate to put in the line of classic Welsh half-backs'. Carwyn James subsequently won two Welsh caps and became a rugby coach of unparalleled wisdom and flair. His finest hours were the occasions when the British Lions XV of 1971 and Llanelli in 1972 defeated the powerful All Blacks. In contrast, Siân Phillips, also a native of Carmarthenshire, gained an honours degree in English at Cardiff before embarking on an illustrious career in theatre, film and television. This distinguished actress, who was awarded an honorary D.Litt. by the University of Wales in 1984, is pictured

213

214

215

here in the role of 'Vera' in *Pal Joey* at the Albery Theatre (*Plate 214*). In her youth, she recalled, the advantages of higher education were proclaimed 'with evangelical zeal' by her parents, and 'underpinning every domestic argument was the grim and poignant reminder that one's education was the only thing that could not be taken away from one in a world that within living memory in South Wales had shown itself to be bleak and unfeeling'. A third example is Neil Kinnock, a miner's son from Tredegar who was elected leader of the Labour Party in 1983 and who, in 1992, came close to becoming the first graduate of the University of Wales to enter 10 Downing Street as Prime Minister. Although Neil Kinnock's academic record at Cardiff, where he studied industrial relations and history, was lamentable, he won many admirers as a fiery public speaker. In 1965 he was elected President of the Students' Union, having based his campaign on the slogan 'Kinnock for Efficiency, Initiative, Approachability, Experience'. In a pen-portrait of him in *Broadsheet* in 1963 (*Plate 215*), one of his colleagues wrote: 'Being with Neil is like being near a steam engine. One has a general impression of tremendous energy, but there is a hell of a lot of noise too.' In July 1992 Neil Kinnock received an honorary doctorate of law from the University of Wales.

THE PERIOD from 1947 to 1975 has been recently described by Lord Annan as 'the golden age of the don', an age when the cultivated, many-sided lecturer was not only idolized by his students but also held in public esteem. Probably the most distinctive, popular and lively professorial figure in the academic world in Wales was E. G. Bowen (*Plate 216*), who served the cause of geography and anthropology at Aberystwyth for nearly forty years. In his navy-blue suit and black homburg hat, he cut a familiar figure in College circles, and his tiny frame gave no hint of his enormous reserves of energy. One of nature's enthusiasts, he was one of the most animated and attractive lecturers in the University. His introductory lecture to freshers (delivered annually in spite of persistent, but good-natured heckling) was a highlight in the student calendar. Like A. J. P. Taylor, he had the uncommon knack of being able to communicate his ideas and enthusiasm to people from all walks of life. He could lecture on a wide range of topics – the Celtic saints, drovers and seafarers, Welsh Baptists, and superstitions – and his vivid presentation was redolent of the techniques employed by ancient Welsh story-tellers. He once said: 'My audience is a family. I'm not speaking at you or to you but with you. This is very much in the Celtic tradition.' E. G. Bowen's contribution to the reputation of historical and cultural geography at Aberystwyth was immeasurable and two years after

216

217

his retirement in 1968 a richly deserved honorary D.Litt. was conferred upon him by the University of Wales. When he died, aged eighty-two, in 1983, many felt that a large part of the ethos of the University of Wales perished with him.

One of E. G. Bowen's most colourful colleagues was also a diminutive man (always with a bow-tie), who served the College at Aberystwyth for the best part of forty years. D. Gwenallt Jones (1899–1968) – known universally as Gwenallt (*Plate 217*) – was a major Christian poet. His first volume of poetry, *Ysgubau'r Awen* (The Sheaves of the Muse) (1939) created a stir and established his reputation as a forthright and sometimes scathing critic. Four major volumes followed (including *Y Coed* (The Trees) posthumously published in 1969), each of which included poetry which was 'as tough as wrought iron'. He used to glide into lecture rooms as though casters were fixed to his feet, and his students relished his Chaplinesque humour and the caustic manner in which he stripped bare the humbug, cant and philistinism of contemporary Wales. A conscientious objector and a passionate nationalist, Gwenallt was a man of resolute convictions. As R. S. Thomas wrote:

218

> ... Watch him,
> As with short steps he goes.
> Not dangerous?
> He has been in gaol.

In 1967 he was awarded an honorary D.Litt. by the University of Wales in recognition of his distinction as a poet, literary critic and teacher.

No member of staff better personified the inter-Collegiate spirit than Professor Gwyn Jones (1907–) (*Plate 218*), who graduated in English at Cardiff in 1928, served as lecturer in his old College 1935–40, filled the Chair of English Language and Literature at Aberystwyth 1940–64 and then the Chair of English Language and Literature at his Alma Mater 1965–75. A marvellously gifted and prolific scholar, novelist and short-story writer, Gwyn Jones has recently been described as 'a man whose heart is in Wales, but whose head allows him to range freely across the wider world'. An international authority on the Vikings, he has also written extensively on the Mabinogion and Anglo-Welsh literature. His services to the arts, especially to literature, in Wales have been truly outstanding, and the honorary D.Litt. conferred upon him by the University of Wales in 1977 and the Cymmrodorion Medal in 1991 are just some of the major honours which he has received in recent times. There are few scholars whose books are as widely read for pleasure as for intellectual stimulation, and those who studied under Gwyn Jones speak of him with great admiration and respect.

By the 1980s, old-style, devoted scholars, teachers and populists of this kind were a dying breed. Gone, too, were the days of the absent-minded professor and the gifted eccentric. An age which prized efficiency, enterprise and philistinism above all else had arrived, and not a few dons in the University of Wales were understandably loath to welcome such a brave new world.

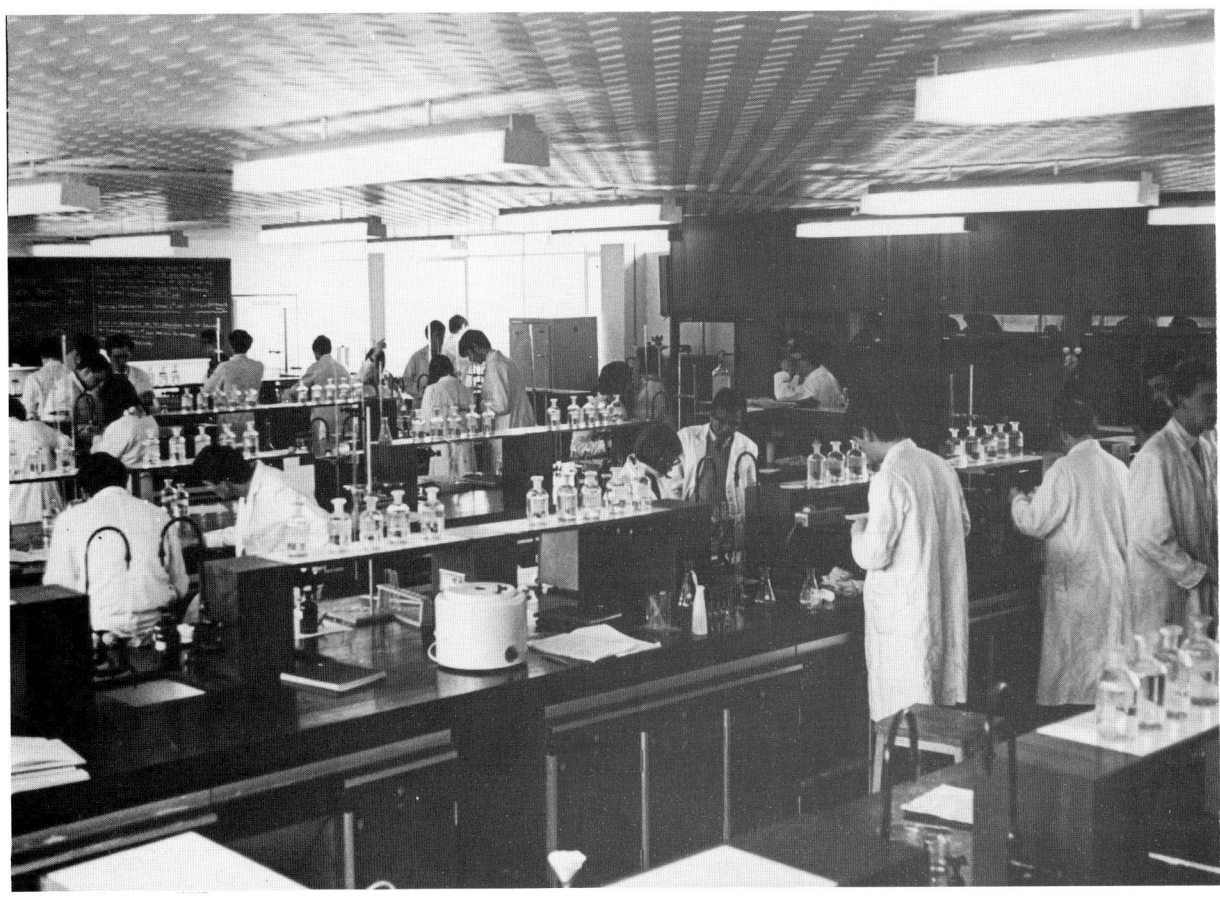

219

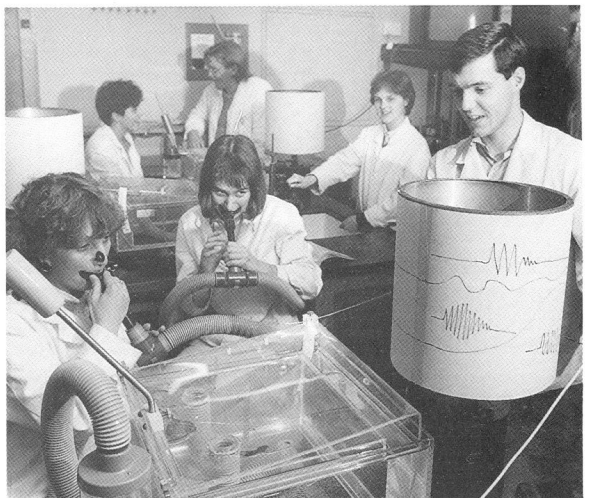

220

As the world changed in the post-Robbins years, so too did the curriculum and research of universities. There was irrefutable evidence that the neglect of technological education had left Britain trailing far behind its foreign competitors. Strong pressure was exerted on the University of Wales to produce scientists and engineers as well as ministers and schoolteachers. The twin forces of democracy and technology were changing people's ideas about the functions of universities and casting doubt on the cherished notion of permitting students to acquire 'learning for the sake of learning'. As a result, the University of Wales became more responsive to its duty to act as a nursery of scientists, technocrats, metallurgists, doctors and engineers. The provision of new and sophisticated laboratories and research facilities helped to attract high-quality students (Plates 219–20). By 1970–1, when the total number of full-time students had soared to 14,832, students pursuing scientific subjects (27.8 per cent pure science, 15.6 per cent applied science) were more numerous than their arts-based colleagues (26.6 per cent arts, 13.5 per cent economic and social studies).

NOT SURPRISINGLY, Welsh Colleges began to take the initiative in original scientific research. Great strides were made in the post-Robbins era, particularly as departments responded positively to the need to forge intimate links with research work carried out in industrial laboratories and in the world of technology in general. From the 1970s onwards complex, advanced and expensive equipment and facilities, like the electronic microscope used to study the structure of animal cells (Plate 221), the receiving antenna for research into the physics of the ionosphere (Plate 222), and the interaction of laser radiation with gases (Plate 223) were introduced. Expansion in research provision and in postgraduate training followed, and collaborative research programmes with science departments in Europe and America strengthened and enriched existing courses and provided students with valuable international contacts.

221

222

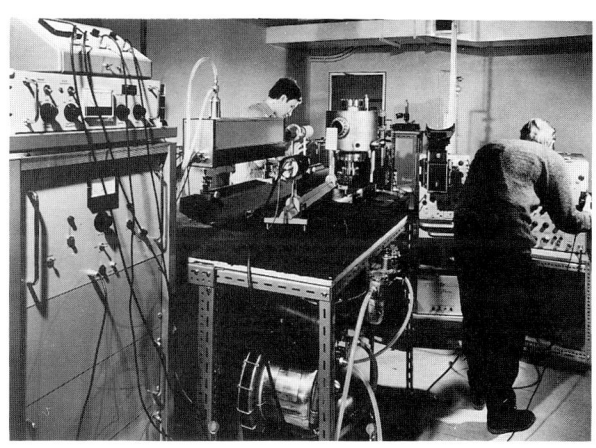

223

THE QUEST for scientific excellence, at least among the staff of the University of Wales, soon bore fruit. By 1977, there were eight Fellows of the Royal Society at Aberystwyth, six of whom (from left to right) – Professor P. F. Wareing (botany), Professor (Sir) Granville Beynon (physics), Professor (Sir) J. Meurig Thomas (chemistry), Professor Emeritus Gwendolen Rees (zoology), Professor J. S. Anderson (chemistry) and Professor J. P. Cooper (Director of the Welsh Plant Breeding Station) figure in *Plate 224*. In 1978 Bangor, too, had good cause to rejoice in the success of its four Fellows of the Royal Society. These richly deserved awards reflected the success of the University in training and attracting distinguished academics and providing them with an exceptional range of modern equipment and instrumentation.

224

ONE OF the most striking features of the post-Robbins phase was the impact of high technology and, in particular, some quite extraordinary advances in the theory and application of computer systems. The development of the computer revolutionized higher education, especially following the publication of the Flowers Report (1966) on computing in universities. Colleges vied with one another to adopt the most advanced computer and digital systems, and *Plates 225–7* are a salutary reminder of the astonishing acceleration of computer technology in our times. By the late 1980s (*Plate 228*) microcomputers were being used extensively as part of the teaching process and as a means of serving the educational and vocational needs of students. Even dyed-in-the-wool arts-based members of staff have of late begun to develop an aptitude for database management, numerical analysis, and image processing. Although nothing can replace the influence of an intellectually gifted and inspiring teacher, there is no doubt that computer systems have transformed the pursuit and organization of knowledge.

225

226

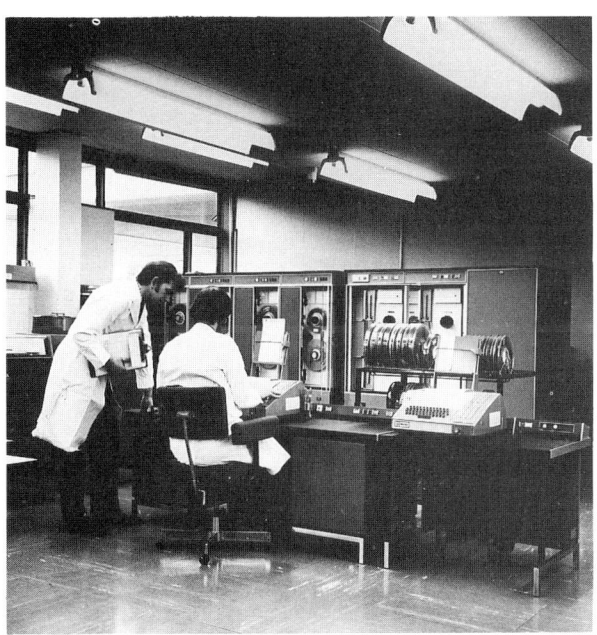

227

228

AN IMPORTANT and perhaps inevitable consequence of the programme of expansion of staff and student numbers was renewed interest in the administrative structure of the University and a growing, but not widespread, desire to defederalize. Proposals for the defederalization of the University were placed on the agenda and on 16 December 1960 the University Court appointed a University Commission to 'review the functions, powers, and administrative structure of the University and its constituent Colleges and the Welsh National School of Medicine, and to look into the future status of those institutions'. The Commission's deliberations, however, were vitiated by internal dissension and acrimony. The whole matter, as *The Times* put it, became 'a trial of strength'. Defederalists insisted that a federal university was an anachronism, that ultimate power already lay with the constituent elements, and that the creaking administrative machinery of the University was the cause of duplication, delay and intolerable frustration. Pro-federalists retorted that the University was a symbol of the cultural and national unity of Wales, and that dismemberment would create four marginalized and impoverished 'Welsh redbricks'. After an unforgivably long delay the Commission produced two radically different Final Reports. The first, endorsed by fourteen members of the Commission (including Principal Charles Evans of Bangor, Principal J. H. Parry of Swansea and Principal Anthony Steel of Cardiff), recommended the creation of four unitary universities in place of the federal University. The second report, endorsed by twelve members, all of whom were elected representatives of University bodies, called for internal reforms but declared in favour of the federal system. The second report, which bore the unmistakable imprint of the acute powers of reasoning of Alwyn D. Rees (*Plate 229*), Head of Extra-Mural Studies at Aberystwyth, proclaimed that the University of Wales was 'a source of inspiration and pride to generations of Welsh men and women, and is inextricably bound up with their sense of nationhood'. The fourth Principal, Thomas Parry of Aberystwyth, failed to sign either report and outlined his special reasons in a statement published in the Final Report. In April 1964 the University Court – by a majority of seventy votes – supported the conclusions of the Second Report and, much to the chagrin of the defederalists and the editor of the *Western Mail*, gave an overwhelming vote of confidence to the federal structure.

229

THE REMARKABLY swift expansion in student numbers from the early 1960s onwards gave rise to what might be called the student estate. Socrates' 'rebellious youth' responded instinctively to rapid changes and in particular to signs of inequality and oppression. The views of Marx, Castro, Che Guevara and Mao were widely canvassed, and there was much noisy disruption as students became both doughty opponents of injustice and active instigators of change. Demonstrations, sit-ins and strikes over matters ranging from Vietnam to women's rights and racial equality to nuclear disarmament brought much unfavourable publicity to the Welsh Colleges but also revealed that students were acutely aware of moral dilemmas and were developing a lively social conscience. Although to some degree student grievances were imported from abroad, that was not the case as far as the special claims of the Welsh language were concerned. Welsh-speaking students were particularly prone to turbulence, especially when it became manifestly clear that the expansion of higher education meant appreciable numbers of non-Welsh students. In February 1962 Saunders Lewis delivered an extraordinarily powerful lecture, entitled 'Tynged yr Iaith' (The Fate of the Language), on the BBC Home Service. Lewis declared that 'nothing short of a revolution' was required to 'restore the Welsh language in Wales today'. This rousing battle-cry inspired the foundation of Cymdeithas yr Iaith Gymraeg (The Welsh Language Society) in August and a campaign of non-violent civil disobedience designed to extend the use and improve the status of the Welsh language. Young middle-class Welsh students, burning with a fierce pride in their native land and language, became militant activists. In February 1963 dozens of students from Aberystwyth and Bangor held a demonstration at Trefechan Bridge, Aberystwyth and, much to the fury of trapped motorists, sat five deep across the road (*Plate 230*). The campaign for parity of status for the Welsh language had begun.

230

THE TREFECHAN protest was simply the first of a long series of demonstrations, sit-ins, hunger strikes, vigils and sign-daubing activities on Welsh campuses. Many students, the most prominent of whom between 1963 and 1980 were Geraint Jones, Emyr Llywelyn, Ffred Ffransis and Angharad Tomos, were fined and imprisoned for acts of disruption and civil disobedience. As the expansion in student numbers proceeded, so the percentage of Welsh students, especially Welsh-speaking students, declined appreciably:

	1938–9	1958–9	1968–9
Aberystwyth	93	72	44
Bangor	91	49	24
Swansea	100	74	42
Cardiff	96	76	40

Members of the academic staff who cherished the distinctive heritage and traditions of the Welsh Colleges also began to feel a deep sense of alienation towards a University which opened its doors widely to non-Welsh students and which recruited the bulk of its staff from outside Wales. In the editorial columns of *Barn*, Alwyn D. Rees declared that the expansion programme was disastrously short-sighted and damaging, while the views of J. R. Jones, Professor of Philosophy at Swansea, on Welsh nationality and 'the interpenetration of land and language' caught the imagination of both Welsh staff and students. As one acolyte observed: '[he] taught us to see the death of the language as something not merely sad or regrettable but as a matter of the highest seriousness, as a symptom of the crisis of civilization.' Mindful of such matters, prominent Welsh lecturers joined student protesters in mounting a silent vigil outside the main College buildings at Bangor on 7 November 1963 (*Plate 231*).

231

Slowly and often grudgingly, College authorities began to move towards a bilingual policy in administrative matters and to respond favourably to legitimate demands by Welsh-speaking students for specially designated Welsh hostels. Even so, a petition submitted to the College Council at Aberystwyth in 1967, calling for the formation of a Welsh hall of residence, aroused fierce opposition and cries of 'linguistic apartheid' and 'Welsh ghetto' from members of staff who should have known better. None the less, in October 1968 two halls of residence – Ceredigion and Neuadd Davies-Bryan – became bilingual institutions. Five years later, Pantycelyn Hall, named in 1951 after Wales's most celebrated hymnist, was transformed into a mixed hostel for Welsh-speaking students and those who were eager to learn the language. Neuadd Pantycelyn in due course became the most flourishing and successful Welsh-medium hall of residence in the University of Wales (*Plate 232*).

232

IN THE SUMMER term of 1969 Prince Charles, the heir to the throne, enrolled as a student at Aberystwyth and made his home in Pantycelyn Hall. Prior to the forthcoming Investiture at Caernarfon in July, it was thought prudent to afford the Prince the opportunity of learning about Wales, its language, history and traditions. He pursued an intensive course in the Welsh language (*Plate 233*) and many years later, when he recorded his experiences of life at Aberystwyth, he particularly recalled running the gauntlet of student demonstrations and the 'heart-stopping horror of addressing 8,000 people, in Welsh, in a vast marquee at the Urdd Eisteddfod'. During his sojourn at Aberystwyth the Prince was regularly lampooned in Welsh publications, notably the irreverent monthly magazine *Tafod y Ddraig* (The Dragon's Tongue) (*Plate 234*), and Dafydd Iwan, a graduate of the Welsh School of Architecture and Chairman of the Welsh Language Society at the time, composed and sang catchy, satirical songs like 'Carlo' and 'Croeso 69' which were declaimed with great gusto on Welsh campuses.

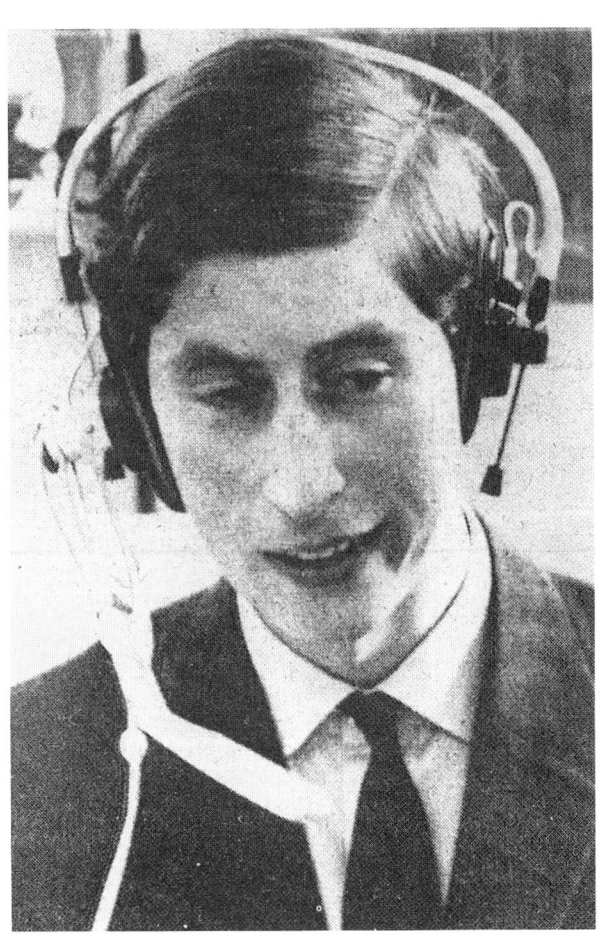

233

234

BY THE EARLY 1970s, students had become the indisputable driving force behind the increasingly militant activities of Cymdeithas yr Iaith Gymraeg. Fired by the slogan – 'Cenedl heb Iaith, Cenedl heb Galon' (A Nation without a Language is a Nation without a Heart) – they were outraged when Lord Hailsham, the Lord Chancellor, having declared that the only thing which differentiated members of the Welsh Language Society from 'the baboons of the IRA' was 'a difference of degree and not of kind', visited Bangor on 29 July 1972 to berate magistrates who were reluctant to share his prejudices. Over 800 demonstrators, mostly students, gave the Lord Chancellor a dusty reception outside the Prichard-Jones Hall (*Plate 235*).

235

PARITY of status for the Welsh language at the College in Bangor proved difficult to achieve, largely because Principal Charles Evans was less than zealous in his devotion to things Welsh. In the student publication *Ffenics*, one correspondent maintained that the Principal 'considered Welshness in this enlightened age a heavy millstone dragging clumsily around the neck of the College'. The decline in the proportion of students from Wales at Bangor (from 72 per cent in 1947 to 20 per cent in 1980) was deeply alarming, and militant students began to wage a war of attrition against obdurate College authorities. 'Welsh Not ar y Bryn' (Welsh Not on the Hill) was a popular slogan in the period 1976–8 (*Plates 236–7*), and in November 1976 four leading officials of the Cymric were sent down following a protest during which administrative quarters were occupied, slogans painted on walls, and English-only documents burnt publicly in the Quad.

236

237

IN ONE SENSE, the expansion of student numbers brought a disguised blessing to those who were mindful of the University's responsibility to preserve and strengthen the Welsh character of its constituent Colleges. It prompted the University authorities to strive more earnestly to satisfy the growing demand that the Welsh language be used as a medium of instruction over a wide range of subjects. In 1962 the University Board for Welsh Medium Teaching was established in order to develop and co-ordinate the appointment of qualified Welsh-medium teaching staff. By 1991–2, a total of thirty-four members of the teaching staff, largely located at Aberystwyth and Bangor, held posts created by the Board which carried a special responsibility for teaching through the medium of Welsh. In 1980 the Board launched one of its most exciting and pioneering schemes of study: this was an external degree through the medium of Welsh at Aberystwyth. Based on the internal syllabus and taught largely by permanent members of staff, the scheme offers courses in Welsh, Welsh history, drama, music, Breton and Religious studies, and caters for mature students studying on a part-time basis (*Plate 238*).

238

IN OCTOBER 1985 the University of Wales reaffirmed its reputation as the custodian of Welsh ideals and aspirations by establishing the Centre for Advanced Welsh and Celtic Studies under the directorship of Professor R. Geraint Gruffydd (*Plate 239*). Financed by a special grant from the University Grants Committee, the Centre was located in Aberystwyth but administered by the University. The aim of this new Welsh institution was to foster collaborative research in Welsh language and literature, the history of Wales, and other Celtic languages and literatures. The Centre's first five-year project, research into the work of the Gogynfeirdd (the Poets of the Princes) *c*.1100–1283, established its reputation as a centre of excellence in the field of Celtic scholarship, and by the time a permanent home for the Centre, on the site of the National Library of Wales, had been completed by November 1992, a second project on the social history of the Welsh language had been launched.

239

ONE OF THE most gratifying consequences of the unprecedented scale of expansion in student numbers in the post-Robbins era was the increasingly cosmopolitan nature of the University of Wales. As Welsh and non-Welsh students found themselves mixing with people from a rich variety of backgrounds, the campuses became lively and tolerant international communities. The proportion of overseas students increased from 4.7 per cent in 1958–9 to 9 per cent in 1975–6, and by 1992 students from 118 countries outside the United Kingdom were represented in Welsh Colleges. Among the most valuable services available for overseas students are English-language training classes for those who are eager to improve their proficiency either before or during their courses at university (Plate 240). Growing numbers of mature students from abroad (Plate 241) many of whom bring experience, motivation and commitment to the Colleges, have helped the University to achieve a world-wide reputation. Nor is the traffic one-way. The European dimension looms much larger in teaching and research programmes and the ERASMUS (European Action Scheme for the Mobility of University Students) scheme has broadened the experiences of Welsh students by exposing them to other languages and cultures.

241

240

THE PROVISION of residential accommodation for as many students as possible either on, or in close proximity, to the College campuses became a pressing need in the post-Robbins era. Traditional halls of residence, which had always prided themselves on their distinctive, but somewhat old-fashioned style and atmosphere were now joined by 'skyscraper' hostels like Neuadd Sibly at Swansea (*Plate 242*), which provided friendly and relaxed places in which to live and work. Aberystwyth established an integrated complex of residences at Penbryn where four units, each named in memory of major figures associated with the College, offered well-equipped and comfortable study-bedrooms (*Plate 243*). Increasingly, however, those students who preferred a more independent and self-reliant style of living moved out of the traditional hostels and either settled in bed-sitting rooms and flats, or self-catering houses where communal facilities, usually grouped around a kitchen and dining area, were available. *Plate 244* shows the Mackintosh Place Residences built in Cardiff in 1983. Another solution was the creation of student villages. The pioneer here was Swansea: in 1964 the College acquired Hendrefoelan House, formerly the home of Lewis Llewelyn Dillwyn, together with 121 acres of land, which became the location of an imaginatively constructed student village offering private housing units grouped in twos, threes and fours for 1,400 students (*Plate 245*). Of every 100 students in the University of Wales in 1957–8, twenty-six lived in hostels, fifty-five in lodgings, and nineteen at home. By 1974–5, of every 100 students, forty-four lived in hostels, forty-eight in lodgings, and eight at home. Nowadays each College attaches the utmost importance to the provision of good quality accommodation, not only in order to meet the needs of students but also the expectations of vacation conferences.

242

243

244

245

EXPANSION in higher education also encouraged the development of modern, purpose-built Students' Union buildings (*Plate 246*), headed by groups of full-time student sabbatical officers who administer a wide range of commercial activities (including bars, cafes, banks, shops, concerts and discos), confidential welfare services, community action groups, telephone counselling services, and playgroups, as well as flourishing and diverse arts activities.

246

247

THE EXPANSION of student numbers was also accompanied by (and perhaps even led to) greater permissiveness, and what John Aubrey used to call 'juvenile impetuosity'. The Swinging Sixties ushered in the twist, Beatlemania, long hair, flower power, the protest songs of Pete Seeger, Bob Dylan and Joan Baez, and rock concerts. Hair began to creep down to the shoulders of female students, and hemlines crept upwards (Plates 247–8 reveal differences in fashion between students at Carpenter Hall, Aberystwyth, in 1949–50 and 1964–5). Gael Greene's *Sex and the College Girl* was published in 1964 and the Family Law Reform Act, implementing the recommendations of the Laity Report, lowered the age of majority from twenty-one to eighteen as from 1970. Under this onslaught, vestiges of the old puritan code of conduct swiftly vanished.

248

As the issue of parity of status for the Welsh language engaged the minds and hearts of growing numbers of Welsh students, so did the Inter-College Eisteddfod flourish. A much wider range of competitions and activities was organized and students gifted in poetry, literature and traditional song were joined by those with expertise in arts and crafts, photography and drama. Raucous pop groups (*Plate 249*), and jazz entertainment brought greater variety – and noise – to the festival.

249

250

F OUNDED in 1974 in order to articulate the demands and defend the interests of students in Wales, UCMC (Undeb Cenedlaethol Myfyrwyr Cymru) or NUS Wales has organized high-profile campaigns against cuts in public spending, the introduction of student loans, the freezing of grants, the Poll Tax, and disentitlement to social security assistance such as housing benefit. It has also vigorously represented the views of students on the status of the Welsh language, environmental matters, women's rights, and international issues (*Plates 250–1*).

GWRTHDYSTIAD CENEDLAETHO

YN ERBYN DYLED MYFYRWYR

NATIONAL DEMONSTRATION

AGAINST STUDENT DEBT

251

252

253

One of the major consequences of the expansion in student numbers was the higher level of participation in physical and recreational activity on Welsh campuses. An outstanding range of modern facilities in the form of sport centres, all-weather pitches and multi-gyms now cater for traditional sports like association football, hockey and rugby, while each of the Welsh Colleges can boast ideal surroundings and facilities for mountaineering, pot-holing, sailing, canoeing, parachuting and hang-gliding (*Plates 252–3*).

254

255

256

Although each College has an active and vigorous Rag Society, Aber Rag reigns supreme as the most successful Student Charity Appeal in Europe. Its success over the years has been based on large-scale distribution and sales of an irreverent (and often unashamedly sexist) magazine (*Plate 254*), colourful rag processions, public auctions, pram races (*Plate 255*), and several highly imaginative publicity-seeking stunts and hoaxes. The most memorable hoax occurred in February 1966 when Peter McInally, a Visual Art student, smuggled a fake self-portrait by a certain 'Givitto Aberragi (1560–1638)' into the National Gallery and contrived to hang it in a space left by the removal of another painting. Much to the glee of Aberystwyth students, ten days elapsed before the 'interloper' was discovered by the authorities at the Gallery. Such escapades regularly raised the profile of Aber Rag and have enabled Aberystwyth students to donate more than £2 million to a wide range of national and international charities since 1947 (*Plate 256*).

AFTER 1973–4 the dramatic expansion of the post-Robbins period ground to a halt. During the OPEC crisis of 1973 large reductions in public expenditure were announced and the universities of Britain suffered a crippling 10 per cent reduction in their resources. Serious underfunding and a dearth of capital resources imposed severe constraints on planning and bred an acute sense of uncertainty. Worse was to follow. The advent of Thatcherism in 1979 set in motion a programme of planned contraction. When savage financial cuts were announced by the UGC in July 1981, Lampeter's entry in the Annual Report of the University epitomized the widespread feeling of apprehension and betrayal: '"The Lord giveth, the Lord taketh away: blessed be the name of the Lord". Job's words, *mutatis mutandis*, might be aptly applied by the College to the University Grants Committee.' Harassed dons were forced to come to terms with the fact that academic tenure was not simply confined to the leisurely pursuit of knowledge and truth. College authorities were increasingly preoccupied with penny-pinching economies, freezing posts, re-deploying staff or encouraging them to apply for early retirement. Desperate efforts were made to economize without affecting academic standards, but the morale of staff and students plummeted sharply. Council chambers and common rooms echoed to phrases like 'maximum efficiency', 'staffing ratios' and 'selectivity exercises'. The 1980s were particularly testing years for Cardiff. Its Principal, Cecil (Bill) Bevan (*Plate 257*) imprudently (though some claimed heroically) took a political stand against the strict cash-limit conditions imposed by the Government by committing the College to a period of unbridled expansion. As early as January 1974 Bevan had

257

declared: 'We want to expand like hell.' But reckless expansion and serious financial and administrative mismanagement brought the College to the very brink of insolvency in 1987, and the crisis was averted only when the Government bailed out the College by granting it the sum of £10 million to facilitate large numbers of early retirements and voluntary severances and to set in motion major academic reorganization. Principal Bevan – mulishly stubborn to the last – retired in March 1987 under a cloud of controversy. He died in April 1989.

EVEN AS he saved the College at Cardiff from bankruptcy in the summer of 1987, Sir Peter Swinnerton-Dyer, Chairman of the University Grants Committee, made it clear that the price to be paid was expeditious merger with its neighbour UWIST. In July an Executive Commission and Management team was set up to prepare for the formal establishment of a single, merged institution comprising University College Cardiff and UWIST. The necessary details were hammered out within a single session and the University of Wales College of Cardiff was born on 26 September 1988. Its first President, Lord Crickhowell, former Secretary of State for Wales (1979–87), was presented with the Royal Charter by G. I. de Deney, Clerk of the Privy Council Office (*Plate 258*). The President voiced the view that 'for even the larger institutions, to aim for comprehensive independence would be folly', while the newly-appointed Principal, Dr (later Sir) Aubrey Trotman-Dickenson, with abrasive self-assurance, declared that 'God is on the side of the big battalions'.

258

Impelled by the implications of the Jarratt Report on Efficiency Studies in Universities (1985), together with insistent calls from some of the constituent Colleges for greater independence and flexibility, in November 1987 the University established a review body called The Powers and Functions Group, whose brief was to advise the University Council as how best to make the institution more effective as a federal body. A team of ten was headed by Sir Goronwy Daniel (*Plate 259*), former Permanent Under-Secretary of State at the Welsh Office, Principal at Aberystwyth (1969–79), and one of the most able and distinguished Welshmen of modern times. The working group spent eighteen months producing a consultative report which was accepted by the University Court in October 1989. Sir Goronwy Daniel's message was crystal clear: 'united we stand, divided we fall', and his report unequivocally supported the case for maintaining a federal university. It recommended the establishment of a Joint Planning and Resources Committee under the chairmanship of a Deputy Pro-Chancellor, and the establishment of Inter-Collegiate Boards of Studies to contribute to planning in teaching and research, and to avoid duplication of resources and funds. The Daniel Report was warmly received in many quarters and seemed to herald a new era of co-operation and efficiency.

259

THE INK had barely dried on the Daniel Report when forces of circumstance conspired to strengthen the demand for College autonomy at the expense of loyalty to the University. The Government White Paper on Higher Education (1990), the abolition of the binary line in 1992, and the Higher Education Funding Council for Wales instituted in April 1993, produced a dynamic which propelled the federal structure to the centre of the stage. Such factors were bound to produce serious divergences of outlook and threaten the cohesion of the federal system (Plate 260). Anti-federalists, led by Sir Aubrey Trotman-Dickenson, Principal at Cardiff, railed against a system which allegedly entailed cumbrous and expensive administrative machinery, hampered individual initiatives and progress, and encouraged jealousy and bickering. On the other hand, the new Deputy Pro-Chancellor, Professor Sir John Meurig Thomas FRS (Plate 261), a distinguished Llanelli-born scientist, who was appointed in 1991 to co-ordinate the academic and institutional plans for the University and its constituent Colleges, sought to stamp his own personal style on the reform programme and to foster harmony and goodwill by

260

261

stressing the importance of collaborative endeavour. He called on each College to support a reformed and expanded federal University of Wales which would embody the finest features of its cultural and educational heritage and also reflect the aspirations of its component parts.

In the light of these developments a Working Party, headed by Sir Melvyn Rosser FCA, was appointed by the University Council to reconsider the recommendations of the Daniel Report. It speedily prepared a consultative document which was widely circulated for consideration within the constituent Colleges during the early months of 1993. Given its determination to 'create a spirit of partnership based upon recognition both of the integrity of the Colleges and the University as chartered bodies, and of the unique opportunities within the federal structure to make common cause in selected areas', the Rosser Report may well succeed in resolving the tensions between centripetalists and centrifugalists.

FROM THE early 1990s the University once more was encouraged by Government policy to embark on a programme of expansion. In each of the Colleges planning horizons were lengthened and increased numbers of students admitted. In 1992–3 the number of full-time students in the six Colleges stood as follows:

Aberystwyth	4804
Swansea	6839
Bangor	4803
UWCM	1610
Cardiff	11309
Lampeter	1260
Total:	30,625

In a savagely competitive, market-dominated world, College authorities are increasingly obliged to spend thousands of pounds on designing and producing glossy, full-colour, bumper prospectus editions designed to appeal not only to sixth-form pupils but also to mature, retired or disabled people, non-working women, ethnic minorities and overseas students (*Plate 262*). New modes of teaching – modularization, semesterization and distance learning – appropriate to students from diverse backgrounds are certain to bring about fundamental changes in the manner in which students are taught.

262

263

AT THE time of writing, the precise structure of the University of Wales and its principal officers is in a state of flux. At present it remains a national, federal university comprising six constituent Colleges. Its Chancellor since 1977 is HRH The Prince of Wales, the only former student of the University ever to have filled that office. He is pictured in *Plate 263* in the company (left to right) of Dr Gareth Owen, Vice-Chancellor 1985–7, Dr M. A. R. Kemp, Registrar, and The Right Honourable Lord Cledwyn, Pro-Chancellor, during an Honorary Degree Ceremony held at Swansea in July 1986, and in *Plate 264* in the company of Professor Sir John Meurig Thomas, Deputy Pro-Chancellor of the University.

264

265

THE OLDEST of the six constituent Colleges and probably the most sensible of its historic identity is Aberystwyth. It remains, in Jan Morris's words, 'the symbolic core of Welsh academe'. Most departments have long since abandoned the winding stairways, lofty corridors, turrets and arches of Old College for the new campus which overlooks the town and commands marvellous views of the wide sweep of Cardigan Bay. The new campus has been described by several accredited university guides as 'one of the luckiest university sites in Britain'. The College has always taken great pride in its excellent town-gown relations, and the myriad activities of the Old Students' Association bear witness to its ability to capture and retain the affections of former students. The College motto – 'Nid byd, byd heb wybodaeth' (No world, world without knowledge) – was adopted in 1875 (*Plate 265*), and the College authorities, headed by Principal Kenneth O. Morgan (*Plate 266*), one of the most distinguished and prolific historians of modern

266

267

Britain, remain acutely aware of their obligation to support and foster Welsh culture. Since the National Library of Wales (*Plate 267*) and the Centre for Advanced Welsh and Celtic Studies are located within a stone's throw of the campus, it is not surprising that Aberystwyth has acquired an international reputation as a centre of excellence in Celtic studies. In a bid to encourage change and innovation, significant resources have also been devoted to collaborative work on the environment, drawing on expertise in agricultural sciences, biological sciences, economics, earth studies and atmospheric physics (*Plate 268*). Advances in fields such as applied mathematics, international politics, history and Welsh history, and computer studies have confirmed Aberystwyth's determination to invest, in both human and capital terms, in primary research.

268

NESTLING between the Menai Straits and the rugged peaks of Snowdonia, the University College of North Wales, Bangor, is located in an area of outstanding natural beauty. The campus is still dominated by the imposing Main College building opened in 1911, and the College authorities, headed by the anthropologist Principal Eric Sunderland (Plate 269), are deeply conscious of their obligation and debt to the community in north Wales. Although the number of its Welsh-born students has declined sharply in the post-Robbins era, Bangor has retained a strong sense of camaraderie and fellowship, and has remained true to its motto: 'Goreu Dawn Deall' (The Highest Gift is Understanding) (Plate 270). Among its major assets is the School of Ocean Studies, the largest multi-disciplinary marine science institution in Europe. Striking advances in the study of oceanography have been facilitated by the ocean-going research vessel, Prince Madog (Plate 271), and the College is committed to a programme of intensive research

designed to solve some of the most serious environmental problems of modern times. The Department of Psychology is also determined to become the principal centre for assessing learning processes and language development in children (*Plate 272*). The College is also well placed to promote agricultural and forest sciences, historical and archaeological study, and Welsh scholarship and creative writing.

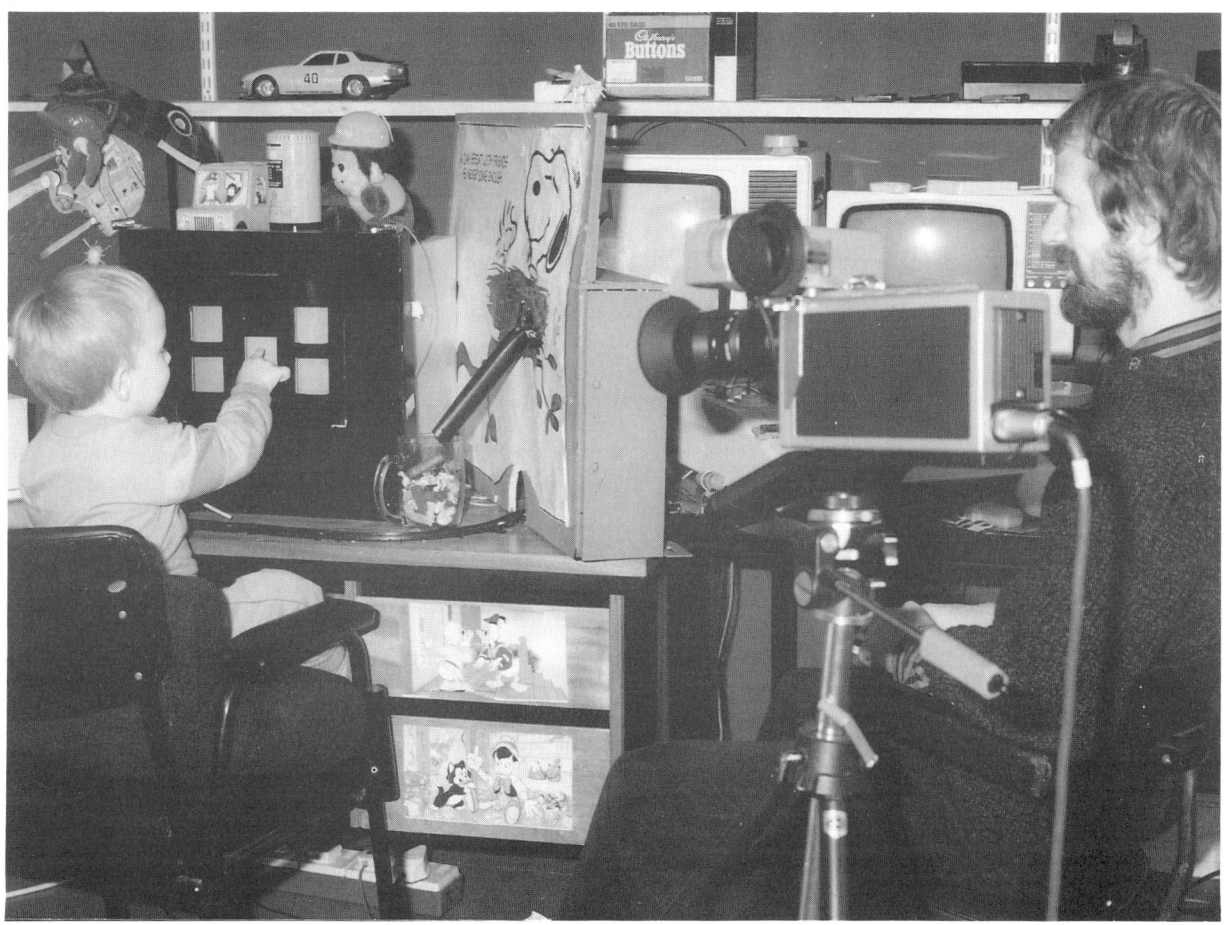

272

273

274

University of Wales College of Cardiff is located in one of the most handsome complex of civic buildings in Britain (*Plate 273*). Cathays Park, with its tree-lined avenues, parks, elegant architecture provides the setting for a progressive, well-resourced modern university which entirely befits a European capital. Guided by its Principal, Sir Aubrey Trotman-Dickenson (pictured in *Plate 274* alongside the statue of Principal J. Viriamu Jones), the College has undergone a radical sea-change since its merger with UWIST in 1988. Not only is it at present the largest of the constituent Colleges of the University of Wales, but it is also a financially stable, forward-looking institution whose rich and diverse degree schemes and research projects are geared to satisfying the requirements of commerce and industry. Several departments, notably the Schools of Engineering, Chemistry and Applied Chemistry, Business Studies, and Earth Sciences, engage in vigorous, pioneering research of international significance. Major programmes of research in solid state physics and astrophysics are in operation in the Department of Physics and Astronomy. *Plate 275* shows students operating molecular beam epitaxy growth systems for making novel semi-conductor structures. Cardiff is pledged to develop collaborative research links with the

202

275

276

industrial and commercial world, and to provide an academic base with a powerful professional and vocational character. It has made no secret of its impatience with the federal framework and it remains to be seen whether its motto – 'Gwirionedd, Undod a Chytgord' (Truth, Unity and Concord) (*Plate 276*) – a maxim plucked from the prayer for the Church Militant in the Book of Common Prayer of 1662 – also applies to the notion of maintaining a unitary University of Wales.

277

278

LOCATED at Heath Park in one of the northern suburbs of Cardiff, the University of Wales College of Medicine is the only medical college in Wales, and its Provost, Professor Sir Herbert Livingston Duthie (Plate 277) is quite properly jealous of its well-earned reputation as a centre of excellence in medicine, dentistry and nursing. The Charter of the College of Medicine declares that one of its major objectives is 'to promote health and welfare with special reference to the needs of Wales'. This ideal is pursued with great vigour and imagination, and the College enjoys close relationships with hospitals and health-care institutions throughout Wales and particularly intimate links with clinical facilities and services in South Glamorgan. One obvious bonus is that undergraduate students in medicine, dentistry and nursing can avail themselves of the opportunity of gaining first-rate clinical experience in a wide variety of environments. The College has a splendid record in attracting research income, and among its major assets are research institutes like the Tenovus Institute for Cancer Research, the Institute for Health Promotion, the Institute for Medical Genetics, and the Institute of Nephrology. Nowhere is the College motto – 'Gwybod, Medr, Iachau' (Knowledge, Skill, Healing) (Plate 278) – together with the special responsibility to cater for 'the needs of Wales', better exemplified than in the Welsh Heart Programme, a community-based project directed by Professor John Catford (Plate 279) and designed to combat and reduce the high incidence of coronary heart disease in heart disease in Wales. Coronary heart disease is a major cause of death in Wales (over 10,000 deaths per annum are attributable to heart conditions), and the College has devoted significant resources to the Welsh Heart Programme in order to heighten public awareness of the links between fat consumption, hypertension, smoking, stress, obesity, excessive alcohol and heart disease.

THE LILLIPUT among the university institutions of England and Wales is St David's University College, Lampeter, whose student numbers totalled 1,091 in 1991–2. Lampeter acquired full College status within the University of Wales in 1988, and its Principal, Keith Gilbert Robbins (*Plate 280*), a well-regarded historian of modern Britain, is committed to expanding student numbers and developing a wider range of subject provision and research facilities. Located in a rural area of sequestered calm and peacefulness, Lampeter is a university where life is quiet, low-key and reassuring. One Student Guide has suggested that its size means that 'it is relatively easy to become a "someone" should you so desire, while it is large enough for you to fade equally easily into the background should that be your wish'. Both the Departments of Archaeology and Geography have established a reputation for

281

280

282

progressive teaching and research, but the pride and joy of Lampeter is its interdisciplinary degree scheme in Religion, Ethics and Western Society. As the College motto declares – 'Gair Duw Goreu Dysg' (God's Word is the Best Learning) (*Plate 281*) – Lampeter can boast a long and honourable tradition of theological and biblical study, but by keeping abreast of modern trends in religious studies it is now able to offer flexible degree schemes which enable students of all religious persuasions to endeavour to understand the challenges confronting religious communities in multi-faith environments throughout the world. The Centre for Islamic Studies, founded in 1988 and heavily dependent on the munificence of the Crown Prince of Abu Dhabi and the Crown Prince of Bahrain, offers a peaceful academic atmosphere in which students may study, meditate upon, and argue about the contribution of Islamic culture and civilization to the pattern of world events (*Plates 282–3*).

283

UNIVERSITY College Swansea, is located two miles west of Wales's second city in a substantial area of attractively landscaped parkland directly adjacent to Swansea Bay and within two miles of the Gower Peninsula. Its degree schemes are diverse and geared to the needs of modern society. Single subject degrees are complemented by courses which link engineering and computing, and modern languages with business studies. Cross-fertilization in teaching and research enable students in the School of Modern Languages (which incorporates French, German, Hispanic studies, Italian, Russian, and Welsh) to assess the multifaceted linguistic and cultural heritage of Europe (*Plate 284*), while the European Business Management School offers a managerial and technological perspective on the European Community. 'Gweddw Crefft Heb Ei Dawn' (Craft is Bereft without Talent) (*Plate 285*) is the College motto, and the pick-axe, hammer and anchor on its coat of arms bear witness to Swansea's traditional expertise in science and technology. It is a

285

284

matter of particular pride to Principal Brian Leonard Clarkson (an engineer himself) (*Plate 286*) that Swansea has retained and developed its international reputation as a centre of excellence in engineering. The School of Engineering consists of five departments (Chemical, Civil, Electrical and Electronic, Materials, and Mechanical). Particularly vigorous and successful schemes of research have been launched by the Department of Materials Engineering, notably in Materials for High Performance, Electronic Materials, Polymers and Composites, and Steel Products (*Plate 287*), each of which is taught and researched by internationally recognized authorities. At no time has it been more propitious for students to embark on training schemes of this kind which equip them with the necessary skills for fruitful and profitable careers in research, industry and commerce throughout Europe.

286

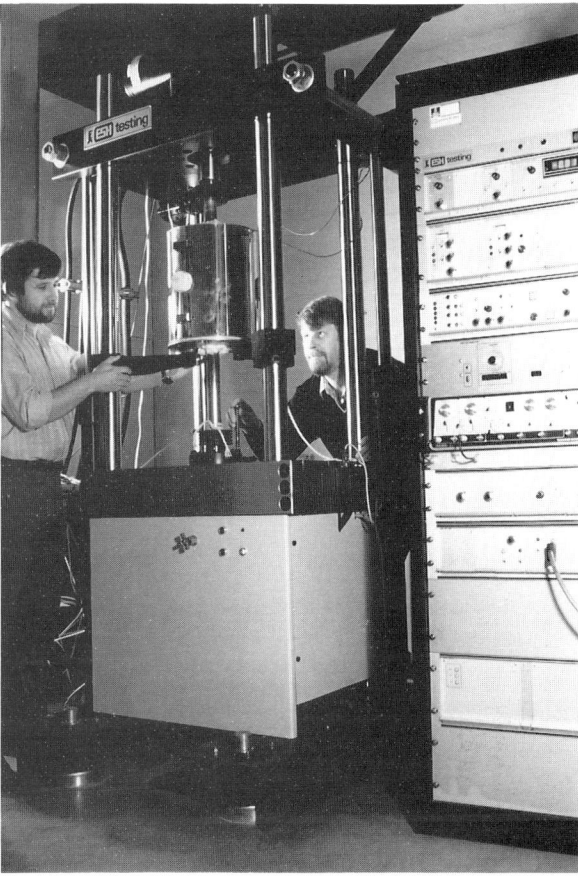

287

AS THE ILLUSTRATIONS and text in this volume bear witness, the University of Wales has expanded and changed enormously over the past hundred years, and only a rash historian would venture to predict what the future holds. It is clear, however, that the University is facing greater challenges than ever before. The combined influence of the massive expansion in student numbers, the abolition of the binary line, and the introduction of new mechanisms for the funding of teaching and research will have profound implications for the future shape, organization and vision of the University. Some are convinced that the federal structure, rather like the Soviet monolith in recent times, will inevitably collapse under the weight of expansionary changes. Several of the constituent parts of the University are determined to acquire greater freedoms and privileges, and are no longer prepared to tolerate a system which, in their eyes, entails wasteful and expensive central bureaucracy and which encourages, at College level, varying degrees of jealousy and cussed delight in mutual hindrance. Conversely, champions of the federal structure maintain that the University is more than the sum of its parts and that any loosening of federal bonds would seriously devalue the degree of the University (*Plate 288* graphically captures the sense of joy and pride of graduates on 'capping day'), consign the smaller constituent units to marginalization and penury, and above all betray aspirations and ideals which are deeply rooted in the history and culture of the people of Wales. It was with a profound sense of pride and conviction that the architects of the University of Wales created a national institution 'in and for Wales' in 1893. Those charged with the responsibility of determining the future structure and role of the University have a daunting assignment, and it is much to be hoped that they will share the sense of mission and commitment which inspired the founding fathers.

288

Acknowledgements

The permission of the following to reproduce illustrations and photographs is gratefully acknowledged:

Cymdeithas yr Iaith Gymraeg: 234

D. J. Bowen: 193, 213

Dyfed Cultural Services Department: 12, 60, 66

Gwynedd Archives Service: 161

Keith Morris: 260, 288

Marian Delyth: 262

Meredydd Evans: 189

The National Library of Wales: 8, 15, 16, 20, 22, 23, 24, 33, 36, 37, 38, 65, 101, 104, 106, 108, 110, 111, 112, 115, 116, 123, 127, 129, 136, 137, 139, 140, 143, 145, 146, 150, 151, 152, 155, 160, 162, 163, 164, 166, 172, 177, 196, 211, 212, 230, 231, 235, 236, 239

The National Portrait Gallery, London: 107

National Union of Students in Wales: 250, 251

Owen Edwards: 9

Prys Morgan: 128, 178

Saint David's University College, Lampeter: 207, 208, 280, 281, 282, 283

Siân Phillips: 214

University College of London: 187, 188

University College of Wales, Aberystwyth: 3, 7, 10, 11, 13, 14, 28, 42, 44, 52, 53, 56, 57, 58, 61, 62, 63, 70, 71, 72, 73, 75, 77, 79, 80, 82, 84, 86, 87, 90, 91, 94, 96, 97, 98, 99, 100, 102, 131, 134, 135, 142, 148, 149, 153, 156, 158, 176, 179, 180, 183, 186, 191, 195, 197, 198, 199, 216, 219, 220, 221, 222, 224, 225, 229, 232, 233, 238, 243, 246, 247, 248, 254, 255, 256, 259, 265, 266, 267, 268

University College of North Wales, Bangor: 4, 21, 26, 27, 30, 39, 40, 41, 45, 46, 47, 48, 51, 59, 64, 68, 74, 76, 78, 81, 83, 85, 88, 89, 92, 93, 95, 103, 105, 132, 154, 157, 159, 165, 173, 174, 175, 190, 269, 270, 271, 272

University of Wales College of Cardiff: 2, 25, 29, 31, 32, 34, 35, 43, 49, 50, 54, 55, 67, 69, 109, 130, 138, 141, 167, 168, 169, 170, 171, 181, 182, 184, 192, 206, 215, 218, 228, 240, 241, 244, 252, 253, 257, 258, 273, 274, 275, 276

University College of Swansea: 119, 120, 121, 122, 124, 125, 126, 200, 201, 202, 203, 223, 226, 227, 242, 245, 249, 284, 285, 286, 287

University of Wales College of Medicine: 117, 118, 204, 205, 277, 278, 279

University of Wales Registry: 1, 5, 6, 17, 18, 19, 113, 114, 133, 185, 194, 209, 210, 237, 261, 263, 264

Welsh Arts Council: 144, 147, 217